CULTIVATING
MAD COW

K A LITTLEWOOD

Matador
9 Priory Business Park
Kibworth Beauchamp
Leicestershire LE8 0RX, UK
Tel: (+44) 116 279 2299
Email: books@troubador.co.uk
Web: www.troubador.co.uk/matador

ISBN 978 1784622 848

British Library Cataloguing in Publication Data.
A catalogue record for this book is available from the British Library.

Printed and bound by CPI Group (UK) Ltd, Croydon, CR0 4YY
Typeset in Aldine by Troubador Publishing Ltd

Matador is an imprint of Troubador Publishing Ltd

For my daughter. I'm sorry you had to go through this.
I love you always, Mum.

Contents

A MACHINE
FOR TURNING
TRAGEDY
INTO ENTERTAINMENT

(PATENT PENDING)
Before operating the unit, please read
the manual thoroughly & retain for future reference.

Tim Etchells *Vacuum Days 2012*

Acknowledgements

Without the support of the following people, getting this book to publication would simply not have been possible:

- To Catherine Carley and the guys at Cafeteria for designing the cover of this book and for being my friend.
- To Ruth Owen for editing this book, for giving me guidance and for believing in me.
- To Wes for your unwavering emotional support and belief in this book.
- To Karen Davies for final proof reading and advice.
- To Phillipa Willits for first edit.
- To Barry White for allowing me to tell this story.

Superhero
April 8th 2004

IT WAS A DOWNHILL TREK from there on in. I fumbled around on the stereo in my little blue Nova, trying desperately to tune in to Radio Sheffield, intrigued to find out how famous I had become.

My newfound fame across the nation brought with it a certain amount of chaos. Things at home had got out of control. The washing was piling up, the cat laid about dehydrated and half starved, the child hanging around street corners getting high and drinking illegal alcohol with her latest mates, trying to work out whether her mother had either gone completely doolally or had really hit the jackpot and become a star. Then my superhero came to my rescue – his name was Barry.

He was a man of great wealth and power. At the age of forty-nine, he stood six feet three inches tall and weighed in at 200 pounds. He had sleek, white hair and big, brown 'come to bed' eyes. Barry White was his name; he was a handsome man with money and power. In fact, Barry was one of the richest and the most eligible men on the entire planet.

Barry White: the occasional playboy, the occasional telephone counsellor. Barry White, sitting there at his desk wearing his 'Barry Can Save The World' suit (actually a jolly sensible single-breasted wool mix number from M&S), he began to fight the greatest threat known to humanity: nasty people.

Unbeknown to Barry, he was about to meet the girl of his dreams, his Barrygirl. She was a beautiful, sensitive, caring young woman who was to become his sidekick and would travel the world fighting crime by his side.

Barry worked for the Justice League of Lala Land, a government-sanctioned group of superheroes.

Of course, none of the above was in the slightest bit true. In reality I knew nothing of Barry. Not a damn thing.

And why would I need to know? After all, it was never going to be about him, it was always going to be about me. Each day I spoke with him on his cosmic glow phone, his soft, tender voice hiding his true emotions; emotions that ran so very wild and deep. A simple, 'Hello you, how are you today?' and I was his, our souls intertwined, our energies pulsating. We were connected; we were soul mates.

Just as the sun continues to shine, like the earth continues to rotate on its axis and the birds continue to sing in the trees in the constant, everlasting sunrise and sunsets: Barry was my miracle.

Barry loved the way that I wrote things, and I wrote loads of things. I wrote to the Prime Minster and told him to 'wake up and smell the coffee you f'ing prick'. I wrote to the head of social services and told them that if they ever came to my house to tell me I am mentally ill again I would put a brick through their f'ing window. Mr Blair's response got lost in the post, and social services ran round like headless chickens wondering what the hell to do with one of their employees who had clearly lost the plot.

I wrote pages and pages and pages of what seemed, to the average Joe, like complete nothingness. I wrote lyrics on toilet walls, I wrote song words on floors, fanatically making sure that every word that came into my mouth was logged somewhere. I wrote a book, which then became a book about a book, and I wrote poetry, beautiful poetry and I wrote policies, poetry and more policies. I sent my writing to important people like MPs, Charles Saatchi, Lionel Richie and the Queen. In fact I sent it to everybody who was anybody. I knew I was a genius and, most importantly, Barry knew it too.

It wasn't long before I got bored with 'other' people and the book that I was writing transformed into being a book about Barry. Barry wasn't boring – quite the opposite – he was a man of mystery and intrigue. Whilst I spent night after night writing about him, he was also writing about me. He agreed that he wrote lots about me, and why wouldn't he? I was one of the Seven Wonders of the World. He was in love with me. We were like one of those couples who shared everything, wore the same coloured anoraks and shared our mushroom and tagliatelle supper; we took on the same persona and, above all, we wrote books about each other. Although my book was a book of love, his looked more like case notes.

Barry was my dream lover, my twin flame, and I knew it from the first moment I heard his voice. From the moment he wrapped his soft dulcet tones around my angry, repressed verbal diarrhoea, wrapping each sentence of mine in a fluffy pink blanket to soothe and soften my harsh, bitter, unforgiving sounds.

It wasn't always happy in our little BT love nest. The eclectic mix of volatile, unsophisticated screaming of obscenities – which could have been mistaken for a rather harsh session with a telephone dominatrix – combined with the gentle, sad, soft puppy droning, ensured Barry was provided with adequate entertainment to keep him from being bored.

Sadly, the 'Tourette's like' symptoms were not confined to just phone conversations with Barry. There were two rather uncomfortable but slightly amusing trips to the nice local police station after having a fairly large, grown-up style tantrum in the local swimming baths at 7am, followed by another similar episode in B&Q two days later – both incidents clearly brought on by a clear case of false advertising – and I decided it best to stay confined to the four walls of my own home. Just Barry and I and, oh yes, I forgot I had a child as well.

Barry seemed to like being abused and thought the whole affair was rather amusing, until it got messy.

'FUCK OFF YOU BIG POO STINKIN ARSEOLE OF A FUCKIN PROFESSIONAL AND JOIN THE OTHER TURDS OUT THERE. THERE IS LOTS OF YOUR KIND YOU'LL FIT IN WELL, YOU MAY EVEN FIND LOVE IN TURD LAND.'

On the odd occasion I would be nice to Barry and share some of my warmer pieces of writing with him:

I never take anything for granted, only a fool takes things for granted, things that are often here today can be gone tomorrow, thats one things that you will never have to worry about with me cos Barry I luv ya just the way you are.

Dont go changing Bazza to try and please me, you've never let me down before. I woudl not leave ya Bazza in times of trouble, i take the good and the bad baza cos I take ya just the way you are, dont be a fashion freak Barry, dont go changing the colour of youre hair, you always have my unspoken passion, even though I might not seem to care. i dont want clever conversation I just want to talk some more. i need to know you will always be the same old Baza that I knew. What will it take Bazza till ya belive in me the way I beleive in you you i diot. i said I loved ya stupid arse, thats forever Darling. i cant love ya more, i love ya the way u are.

Of course nothing was ever spelt right; I was far too important and far too busy writing a book to be worried about inconsequential things like spelling.

Italics and misspellings = Mad Cow

TWO

The Wheel of Misfortune
October 22th 2004

A LARGE TUBE WAS BEING pulled from my throat as I woke
suddenly from a beautiful, peaceful and serene dream, floating
above a bed, light and soft, naked, by the hospital bed of my
grandmother in an old, closed-down ward. There were other
beds that had been made up but lay empty and covered in
cobwebs; the windows were smashed and particles of sunlight
streamed through the tiny holes in the metal fittings that
covered the windows. Granny L was lying on the bed clutching
her knitting needles, knitting a bright blue and pink square,
occasionally smiling up at me. It felt peaceful and warm, safe
and comforting. She had been dead for over twenty years, but
she looked so beautiful, not young, not old, but just like she
had always looked to me, lovely.

'Can you hear me, Kathryn? Do you remember what has
happened?' a voice asked. The room was bright and blurry.
Strong, oppressive lights burned through my corneas, temporarily
blinding me. My throat was sore and my body numb.

'Do you know where you are?' the voice said again. It was
a male voice, a young voice, a voice I was not familiar with.

'I'm in Chapeltown,' I replied, 'I'm dancing and it's all
beautiful.'

'Well, no you're not, actually,' a gentle voice said, cautious and hesitant, delivering the truth of the matter with diplomacy and care. 'I'm afraid you're in hospital, you're in the Northern General Hospital.'

Fragments of memories suddenly started to come together and a sense of complete despair came over me when the abrupt realisation of what had happened registered.

For what seemed like an eternity I drifted in and out of lucidity. The morphine was strong and the more they pumped into me, the more things seemed surreal. Balloons floated in the air, yellow balloons, blue balloons and pink pigs – was it my birthday? Had I given birth? I couldn't remember what was happening? I was scared. There were people talking near my bed, talking about me as if I wasn't there.

'This is Kathryn, she has spinal injuries, a perforated bowel, fractures to both her left and right pelvis and bilateral open comminuted fractures of the calcaneum. There is a strong possibility that she won't be able to walk again.'

It was harsh to listen to. In short, it meant I had fucked it, big time. One guy added, 'At this stage, we are unsure whether she is paralysed.'

I panicked.

Paralysed, oh my god, paralysed! The words slipped so easily off his tongue as if it was an everyday occurrence. Everything else can be fixed, everything else I could live with but being paralysed was a whole different ball game, I wanted it to stop. I wanted to wake up in my bed with the sunlight streaming through my window and pull the cover over my face for an extra half hour. I wanted to be at work dealing with people's dysfunctionalism, I wanted to be with Faye. I wanted anything but this, not this.

There are things in life that happen, things that you do, mistakes you make, some of which can be undone or repaired, like having an affair and subsequently making up, like doing

7

something stupid like drunk driving and losing your licence. And then there are things in life that happen or that you effect and there is no going back. You can't change them, no matter how much you pray, no matter how much money you have or how much love you are surrounded by and this was one of those times. This had happened and there was nothing, not anything in the world I could do to change this situation.

My mouth was dry and the words faint as I tried to speak. 'Faye? Where's Faye? I want to see Faye. Please won't someone help me, I need to see my daughter.' I remembered her going to school on that morning, unaware that her whole life was about to be thrown into complete chaos; that nothing would ever look the same, feel the same or be the same again. Tears ran down my cheek. The voice was there again at my side; I couldn't see his face but sensed his warmth and his fear.

'Loads of people have sent cards for you and you wouldn't believe how many flowers you have! We can't have flowers here in intensive care so your mum took them home.'

This meant that people had been, that people knew about this and I panicked. The embarrassment was overwhelming. I couldn't speak very well but tried to say, 'So that's where I am, intensive care?'.

This was bad, really bad. I knew I wasn't in heaven and I knew this wasn't a dream and I wasn't at home so it made sense that I was here.

The full realisation of what had happened hit me like a ton of bricks. Nausea rose within me, stemming from the fear of the fact that I had survived and I was now uncertain about whether I was, in fact, going to stay alive.

I remembered the ambulance people towering above me when they came to scrape me off the concrete, I recalled them saying to me, 'You're in a bit of a mess aren't you'?

I'd responded by saying, 'Up here' – pointing to my head

– 'is OK, but down there' – pointing to my legs – 'is all a bit fucked up.'

The ambulance man came back to me with, 'I doubt that very much love.' What happened after that I have no idea?

The guy sitting with me was called Sam. He had explained that this was his first time looking after anyone as he was on a school work placement.

I didn't know whether he knew about why I was here, what he had been told or not, and if he hadn't then I didn't want him to know. He seemed too young and fragile for this kind of thing. It would upset him. How could someone so young understand this? How would my own child be making sense of this when I couldn't make sense of it myself? I tried to squeeze his hand but couldn't get my hands to move.

'Shall I read some of your cards to you?'

He began reading, even though I had not given him authorisation to do so.

'This one is from your daughter,' he said, sounding somewhat apprehensive. The words felt like shards of glass penetrating straight through my heart. I couldn't bear to hear this. More tears ran down my cheek and were quickly absorbed into the pillowcase. I wanted him to stop but couldn't say it. 'It says she is really sorry for the way she has been behaving and she wishes now she had been better behaved and kinder and she wants you to know she loves you very much.'

I turned my head in an attempt to move away from the painful words he uttered with emotional detachment, to show that I didn't want him to continue reading. The thought of her pain, her confusion and anguish and fear about what lay ahead in the immediate future was too much to bear. I tried to get up. I was willing God to let me get up to go to her to make it alright. To put my arms around her and shield her, protect her from this. I tried to lift my body but it was not moving. None of my body would move, I could move my fingers and

9

my hands but nothing else and I didn't understand why. Sam realised the agitation that this was causing and decided that it might not be a good idea to read all the cards out this soon.

'Perhaps we will leave the cards for later,' he added placing them back on the table at the side of me.

I had no spatial awareness and everything seemed blurry. Things I could see merged into one big blob. The place, the people, the room and my position within it were all unknown. I didn't know whether someone had removed my contact lenses or whether they were still in my eyes, dried and folded up, painfully hidden under the lids of my eyes.

Having a mild visual impairment since the age of four had made me more aware of smells and touch. Despite being as blind as a bat, I could navigate around places I was familiar with, with some ease. Some of the nurses wore perfume and over the days it became easier to distinguish who was who. Most were nice but one wasn't so nice. It seemed like an eternity on intensive care where no one came, days and days passed by lying on the bed, helpless, frightened, bewildered and completely and utterly dependent on other people.

There were lots of loud noises and machines in the room, most of them wired up to me. The noise from them was constant and making my fragile brain feel like it was about to explode; buzzing and bleeping, alarms and bells all working at the same time, simultaneously, day in, day out. There were clearly other people in the room; seriously unwell people, very sick and wired up to life support machines.

This was the portal between life and death, the gateway to heaven or hell. If my angst had been imagined before, it was now very real. This was where each and every individual who comes to confront the fundamental precariousness of existence, the place where the 'being' is unveiled as being unspeakably fragile and tenuous.

Time moved slowly, days merged into nights. I had no

sense of time or how long I had been here, alone with only staff to care for me. I hadn't seen my family; no one came. I wondered if they couldn't face it or if they had abandoned me. I wondered if they even knew about what had happened. Perhaps they thought I had gone away and they were happier without me there. I wanted to ask but couldn't bear to hear the answer.

I had some vague recollections of Faye being at my bedside. Faye, my fourteen-year-old daughter, sobbing, clinging onto my hand telling me everything was going to be alright. No one else, just her. Her voice was so clear in my head as if she was right here in the room with me now. Her little voice, trying to sound mature and adult, trying to step into the role of the carer and the supporter. Frightened and alone.

Faintly, I remembered feeling her pain and her confusion but was unable reach out to her; couldn't open my eyes or move my body. I'd been shut down, held down with sand bags, but whether they were temporary or permanent I had no idea.

Inside me I was saying, 'Don't cry darling, please don't cry, I am here, I am alive and I am going to get through this,' but the words just wouldn't come out. I felt her pain and thought that I had tried to move my hand onto hers to squeeze it to let her know I was there. Of course this could have been the morphine or a dream but it seemed so real.

If it were true and not just a figment of my imagination, then I was relieved a little that I had been able to let her know, given her a sign that there was hope. I wanted her to know there was hope because there was: it wasn't my time and I was damned if I was going to give up the fight. I wanted to let her know I was here and I loved her and no matter what, I needed her to hang on as I was coming home, very soon.

I was going to fight like hell to get better and out of here to resume my position as her mother, her 'funny mum' and her 'together mum', the mum I had been before all this started.

In this room, I felt very vulnerable and confused, and mistrustful of some of the staff, particularly one of them who I knew didn't like me and she made that clear. Her name was Sally. She set her stall out with me from the inception of our working relationship. She being the carer, me being the cared for. She whispered in my ear on more than one occasion her dislike for people like me: 'wasters of public money', 'a disgrace to society', 'a poor excuse for a mother'. She didn't hide her feelings, and why should she when in here, in this place, she could seemingly get away with anything?

I knew one thing; I didn't need this right now, a bitch fight with a clear advantage. She grabbed my thumb and pushed it hard on the morphine button, telling me to keep pressing it; I didn't want to press the button, it was making me feel sick, I needed to feel the pain, feeling the pain made me feel alive.

Laura was different. She was one nurse I did like. I couldn't see her face but I knew she was beautiful. She smelt like warm summer meadows and she wore Dolce and Gabbana perfume, Light Blue. The intense, sensual smell of jasmine and freesia filled the room when she was around and I knew I was safe in her hands.

She had a kind, warm aura, her hands soft and gentle and her tone soothing. She seemed a little younger than me, probably twenty-eight. She was frighteningly honest. 'You look a right state,' she said bluntly when she had just arrived on shift and came to sit at my side. I liked her openness and honesty.

Keen to sort me out, she got straight to work fixing me up. She was determined she was going to transform me into a Heidi Klum lookalike or, at least, as near as possible. I would have settled for a haircut like Gail Platt compared to how I looked. Not that I had seen how I looked but, given her reaction, it wasn't pretty. Off she trotted on her search around the hospital for some shampoo. My hair was thick and matted with blood, it would need more than just shampoo on it; it needed clippers to chop it all off and start again.

I started to understand the process a little better. Staff seemed to be one-to-one on intensive care, and so for the whole eight-hour shift Laura would be with me, helping me to get better. I tried to tell her that one of the staff members had been very aggressive with me and that I thought she was trying to kill me, Laura asked me who it was and when I tried to explain, she didn't comment. I don't know whether she knew this person had form or whether she just put it down to me being mental. Either way, I was safe with her and for a whole eight hours I could relax in the knowledge that she was not going to turn my machines off and let me fade away, nor tip me off the bed. She was going to give me a makeover. Just how she was going to achieve this seemed unclear at the moment, but she was going to give it her best shot.

She returned with a bottle of Vosene. My heart sank. I hadn't used Vosene since being a child. Vosene was like washing up liquid and I knew that my hair would end up in a big ball of frizz but, being an utter disaster anyway, I was hardly in a position to argue over shampoo. She had run around the hospital to find it and I was most appreciative. I decided to place all my trust in the thought that, when push came to shove, she knew what she was doing. With both her arms under my arms and her knee pressed up against the head of the bed, she pulled and she tugged until I was positioned right at the edge of the bed. It felt good to move into a slightly different position, but my spine felt strange.

'For my next trick,' she laughed, 'I am going to wrap you up in black bags.'

She tore several black bags and covered both me and the bed. I felt like a self-basting turkey about to attend a Halloween party. This was a major undertaking, but a necessary one.

'You might be in a mess,' she added, 'but we might as well

make you a mess with nice hair.' She was certain that by sorting my hair out she could give me a new lease of life, a life-changing sixty-minute makeover. My life needed more than a sixty-minute makeover, it needed a complete overhaul.

The warm water trickled down my neck on onto the plastic, seeping through and wetting the sheets. I didn't care; it was heaven. Her soft hands massaged the shampoo into my scalp, gentle but firm enough to wash the dried up blood away. Her tender approach soothed and quietened my mind, relaxed and peaceful for one brief moment I forgot my predicament. I could have been in the most luxurious salon in the world until I heard a quiet, 'Oops!'

'I don't know what is happening here,' Laura exclaimed, 'it's all gone a bit knotty,' she laughed.

Like all women, I knew my own hair and I knew that Vosene shampoo was dangerous and that it would require a serious amount of good conditioner to put this right. She dried it off, stood back and burst out laughing.

'It's even more matted than I originally thought!' she explained with concern and hilarity. Without a moment to spare she jumped to her feet and ran off to find some conditioner. Her determination to succeed in this mission was admirable. By now I could lift my arm a little and I reached up to feel it.

Like a big clump of straw my hair stood majestically on top of my head, matted and tangled like never before. She came back and presented me with the only thing she could find, 'a conditioning cap'. She carefully read the instructions.

'Warm in microwave?' This to me sounded more like a ready meal than a hair product. 'Put it on head and rub gently,' she continued. 'Sounds simple enough to me,' she said confidently. Laura was enjoying this.

How wrong she was. The cap made the situation worse, ten times worse, and eventually she gave up. Unable to even get the brush through, she began chopping with scissors. So not only had my body expanded to nearly four times its size, not only was it a possibility that I would never be able to walk again and not only did I now have a stoma bag and other absolutely not-ever-sexy things attached to my body, I now looked like Jack Nance from Eraserhead. I was one giant-sized mess.

'How long have I been here, Laura?' I asked.

'About two weeks,' she replied.

'We need that bed,' one of the charge nurses said.

You can have the bloody bed! I thought to myself.

Daily life in intensive care was like a production line; the quicker that you get better, the quicker they shipped you out – either that or you left in a box. Sadly, whilst I was thinking I was on my way home, the reality of the extent of my injuries were unknown to me. This was only the first hurdle. What I thought were plaster casts on my feet and legs were in fact only there to hold my feet together until they decided what to do with them. They had placed me in a coma to stop me from moving and I was only at the start of what was to be a very long and painful journey to recovery.

I wanted to get out of there as much as they wanted me out. It was becoming clearer that I wasn't going to die and that intensive care was no longer needed. Laura was about to go off shift and I was frightened about who was going to be on next. They had hoisted me out of bed and I slid onto the floor. My spine and coccyx bone seemed to be missing. 'Why can't I feel my back Laura? Why can't I sit up straight?' I asked her as she was on her hands and knees in a desperate attempt to untangle the millions of wires attached to my body that followed me everywhere. 'The doctors will explain more to you now you are awake, just try and relax,' she said in her soothing, kind manner.

The doctors did explain later that day and told me that I

was right about the fact my coccyx bone was missing as it was, it had smashed into a thousand pieces and all the pieces were floating around like fragments of smashed china at the base of my spine which was also broken in four places. Sitting was never going to be the same again. I was lifted off the floor and placed back into a chair. I was ready. I was ready to move onto the next phase of the journey: high dependency.

For a few weeks I was completely disorientated, pumped up with meds and flying high. I often thought that I was on the set of *Casualty* as an extra, or studying medicine at university and living in student accommodation. I frequently didn't know whether I was inside or outside the building, on the grass or in the car park, and I still firmly believed that one of the nurses was trying to kill me.

Sometimes, I was a contestant on *Wheel of Fortune*, which was positioned on the wall opposite my bed. The wheel, framed with steel tubes on which tiers of Plexiglas are placed, supported by steel rods, its computerised lighting instruments displaying different colour choices, spinning on its shaft, with its unmistakable sound of the rubber flippers flying past, waiting for it to dish out it *Wheel of Fortune* trick or Treat stakes. I had some of the letters YO - / H - - E / -UC- - D/ -T/ TH - S/ - IME/ - - THR-N.

It didn't take a genius to work that out, and of course I won. Time to spin the wheel: where was it going to land? 'You won't survive this?' or 'You will lose your job and house'?

Or will it be, 'Everyone hates you'? or 'You won't walk again'?

Or will it land on 'Barry loves you', and 'you will live happily ever after'?

Or 'You win two million quid and never have to work again'?

Of course there wasn't a game of *Wheel of Fortune* being played out in high dependency, or any other games shows for that matter. I was on morphine – lots of it – and my mind was playing tricks on me.

The more I longed for none of this to have happened and wished time could have reversed, the more terrifying the situation felt. The nurses came and went, doing their jobs and getting on with their lives. Some had more interesting lives than others; one was an artist and a pianist, one of them was a mother of three, married to a doctor with a home in Spain as well as in England.

Their lives all seemed so functional, happy and normal. I couldn't remember my life being functional and normal because I had been ill for so many years. It had been a good life, but not what some would describe as being 'normal', and my current situation was certainly not normal. It was about as far away from normal as one could get. Now I had no idea how my *Wheel of Fortune* was going to play out. One thing was clear, this was not going away and neither was I.

THREE

Sort-ed
March 12th 2004

FEBRUARY 2004 HAD BEEN a pretty regular month in my life. No real momentous or revolutionary event had taken place, other than the fact I had taken up, single-handedly, the task of building a flat pack, off-the-shelf, Maple Oak finish kitchen that I had begun to assemble piece by piece each night after work. With no boyfriend, no social life, no sitters, no money and a house full of other people's kids day and night, my mundane life plodded along. I had had a fairly eventful life up until that point but my low threshold for boredom was struggling to cope with the 'new me'. Work had won the battle of fun times.

I had embarked on my career as a social worker at the age of thirty having been to university as a mature student. I had left school with only just enough qualifications to scrape through an access course and then university. I had only been in this post since September 2003 and I didn't feel as settled as I did in my previous post on the Looked After Children and Children In Need team in Rotherham. I'd bailed out of Rotherham as things were getting bad. Cases were piling high and staff shortages were chronic. On the team I was working on there were only two qualified social workers, one senior practitioner and around ninety-four cases and we simply could not keep up. There was also much concern around for personal safety, not just from the run of the mill aggressive clients but as some young people on our case load were being sexually exploited by groups of Asian males in Rotherham, the fear for safety was quite significant. They knew who we were and they knew we had informed the police about them. I knew if I didn't bail out it wouldn't be long before they were carrying me out of that place in a coffin so I had left Rotherham and taken a job in Sheffield on the Referral and Assessment team some eight months previous. This proved to be a disastrous move.

What I needed was to come out of front line social work altogether but finding the right job was hard. I loved my work and I thought I was good at it but it was making me sick. Feeling personally responsible for other people's hurts, crippled with anxiety, that I could do so little to effect change, was a lethal combination. Learning to switch off or shut down seemed impossible. Each day a fresh layer of distress built on my already overworked and overloaded brain. The ridiculously busy and emotionally draining job, which paid shit money, did nothing to alleviate my chronic insomnia, which I had suffered from since being a teenager.

Coping from day-to-day became a way of life and only after the six-mile run and several visits to the gym each week, followed by one and a half bottles of red wine each night, did I feel like I could cope and, apart from the red wine, my world became colourless and one dimensional. The continuous diminution in resources and energy, coupled with a doctor who believed that the world's problems would be solved if everyone downed bucket loads of antidepressants each day, had left me in a mess. I needed a break, which I took, but sadly the break didn't go quite as planned.

On that fatal Friday, after being in court with two separate families, two sets of care proceedings where four children were about to become subject to full Care Orders and removed into foster care for long-term placement, subconsciously, I knew that something momentous was going to happen that would mean that I, in all likelihood, would not be returning to that job. For weeks I had spent night upon night writing reports only to find that the solicitor had lost all the paperwork that I had personally taken down to her office. It was quite a momentous cock up on her part as now the judge ordered that I gave verbal evidence, which I just knew I was not in a fit state to do. This, coupled with the fact that my mum had gone into hospital to have a new knee fitted, that day was the straw that broke the camel's back. This was not going to be a holiday, a break for me; this was going to be too much pressure.

Just as I assumed, the two weeks' annual leave did indeed end up being something entirely different from normal people's holidays. Something more fun, something much more scary but whatever was happening during that time, one thing was sure, things were never going to look the same again, I was never going to be the same person again and I was not ever going to return to social work – or so I thought.

I knew I was sick and I also knew society was sick, as 'social care staff' were only ever dealing with the tip of the iceberg of poverty, neglect and abuse. We were shit-shovelers, shoveling the same old shit whilst climbing up the same old, never-ending, impossible shitty, slippy slope of hell and no one outside of the service really gave a toss. The public only cared when something went viral and became national news but failed to see that those things were happening all over the place all the time. The chronic lack of resources meant that little good would ever come of the work any of us did. The lack of appropriate provisions left children and families in ever increasing cycles of poverty and failure and what was needed to do the good long-term preventative work, just didn't exist. The short-sighted views of politicians and policy makers compounded the problem. Pockets of good projects existed outside the service and small local charities, such as Risky Business and One to One Parent, who were usually funded by the church, local community groups or small amounts given to them by the government or lottery money, were under increasing pressure to take referrals for longer term support from us. This whilst the larger, well-resourced charities with their corporate images and polished advertising campaigns and their cash rich bank accounts creamed off more from the stash of cash and contracts whilst doing little to effect change on the ground. Their high thresholds for referrals prevented the support from really getting to the places it needed to be and whilst they cherry picked the easy, less complex, more settled children to work with, the children with the most placement breakdowns, the children who had the most chronic behavior problems, they were the ones who were left out in the cold.

I knew that there had to be a way of making things better, making our communities safer, families less isolated and safer and that if our communities were safer, ultimately children would be more protected and people would need less from services instead of services constantly responding to crisis. I didn't want to continue my career as a shit-shoveler and I sure as hell didn't want my daughter growing up in a world where the gap between the have and have-nots was so wide. I wanted to try and make changes; big changes and a glowing light burning from within me told me that this was possible. This was my calling.

I live in a place called Gleadless – a small township that had sprung up in the late sixties to house the more prosperous working class. Its close proximity to Derbyshire, town and the motorway make it an ideal location. However, Gleadless is a fairly dull place where not much happens. There is a distinct lack of colour – as in cultural mix – because it's a place where the all-white working class aspiring middle class congregate in their semis and where being a single parent is akin to being a witch. I grew up here and I had chosen to come and live back here to raise my own child.

My mate Ralph, who had purchased a home five doors from me several years before, was aware that something was not quite right. Having been friends on and off for the best part of thirty years, we knew each other well. However, our relationship wasn't always a bed of roses. Out of the thirty years we had known each other, on average, we had spent 90% of the time being enemies and 10% being friends, and our relationship often oscillated between looking like a marriage and a murder scene.

He was a sound engineer and musician who prided himself on being cleverer than me, which he was but given my head had not been working right since the age of about five, this was not a hard thing to achieve. My head was so full of exciting, sexy things like child protection, social work and building flat packed kitchens that I had little time for fun and wit and was in danger of becoming a dried up old prune. He was a quick-witted genius who never failed to make me laugh. I'd lost my mojo big time and had become so troubled about everything that I had forgotten how to have fun. We were fast falling into the 90% murder scene period as the sicker I got the more draining on him I became.

Faye was my fourteen-year-old. Despite growing up in a predominantly all-white, heterosexual, semi-middle-class zone, she had been fed on a diet of all things inclusive. My colourful and interesting friends had injected a more realistic interpretation on life and she had many friends who wanted to spend time with us and our relaxed, left of centre views. They had nothing constructive to do or nowhere to go, and most other parents would just leave their kids to their own devices and not care whether they did or didn't return home. As long as they weren't causing them a problem, then that was alright.

Often, I would gather a few of them up and take them off to either North Yorkshire or Dovedale for a camping trip. The kids would pitch their tents in my garden, to my neighbours' disgust, but at least they were safe and not getting into trouble. Each summer, my back garden became a miniature Glastonbury. I didn't mind too much, but as they grew up they were starting to become destructive: garden furniture would get broken and my tents got cigarette burns. They were older than her and weed and drink were becoming common-place amongst them.

There was so much that needed to be done and I had been charged by a higher force to do it. It was my responsibility to society to change things, to speak up for people and I believed that I could single-handedly challenge the government to invest more in our communities, invest more in our children and invest more in front line services. Rather than strip all the good away from our communities, we should all play a part in turning our communities into sustainable and inclusive areas where people care for each other. This would include better services that offered more prevention and support, rather than the existing ones that continuously lunged from one crisis to the next.

My vision was a vision of a central building within my community that everyone would benefit from and feel proud of. A vision of a physical space where old and young could come together and have open communication and learn from each other. A place where children who were living on the margins of society could come and get the help they needed to reintegrate and a place where old people could use their valuable skills to teach younger people and where services could be delivered locally by local people.

As the house prices rose, communities like ours were being stripped of facilities and cohesion. My vision was so brilliant and all-encompassing that it nearly blew my own head off and this vision was going to come to fruition within the next two weeks and if anyone was going to make it happen then I was the person to do so. It was going to be named SORT-ed: 'Sort it out with education'. That was my slogan.

By Saturday I had created several documents with proposals and ideas. My mind was firing on all cylinders.

By Monday morning it was all planned out: I was going to go into work and just quietly and happily would use the council's email to send my proposals across the entire intranet, which included health, education, social care and the police. *No one will believe just how brilliant my ideas are*, I thought to myself as I dressed early in the morning. I made a phone call to my manager at 8am to make sure it was alright to pop into work to use the computer. She was stressing to try and get to work so she didn't ask too many questions. I knew she wouldn't mind and when she saw my genius plan then she would be congratulating me.

I entered Rotter House to weave my magic. My sister, Valerie, had designed me a few logos over the weekend and had emailed them to me, which made the whole thing look particularly impressive.

I sent the first email with several attachments:

I need your help to raise awareness with a group of young people in an area of mixed social status who, like all other young people in our society, are faced with problems that affect their lives.

Children and young people in our area are bored. They are ill informed about things that are presented to them on a daily basis. Drugs for example are easily obtained and distributed openly within the culture of young people in general.

Drugs affect vulnerable young people, if those vulnerable young people do not have the personal resources such as 'self esteem' or good positive friendship networks who will inform someone if they are worried about a friend of theirs. OUR children are often simply not informed or ill informed about substances and their legal status.

So I am taking this opportunity TODAY to write on the behalf of all the young people in OUR area, which is Gleadless, Basegreen and Intake, the area that we chose to live in, to listen to what they need and have to say.

We can choose to ignore this plea for information, help and guidance or we can positively challenge some of the behaviours that OUR teenagers are presenting us with and actively make a big difference for all the young people in OUR area to benefit from YOUR guidance and help.

The phones started to ring as soon as I pressed the send button. I was on floor three and I turned towards the door and ran as quickly as I could towards the lift with a mixture of panic and elation.

Concerned also about the level of exclusions and problems within our three local schools, I decided that the project would link the three comprehensive schools in the area together. It would offer extra support for pupils who have multiple difficulties. I very quickly gathered all my bits of work together and drove around the schools speaking to Connexions advisors, head teachers and learning mentors who all thought the project was an excellent Idea. I'd contacted the media and publicity department at Sheffield City Council and they informed me that the best people who would be able to offer helpful advice and assistance would be BBC Radio Sheffield.

Wasting no time at all, I contacted them and made an appointment with Andy Kershaw, the local radio community news reporter. I'd also approached several businesses in the area to ask for some help with printing and copying material so that I could campaign on a wider scale.

I felt special and excited going to the BBC, and I was amazed at how wonderful their project was. People from all ages were there using their facilities, learning things and setting up projects and businesses as well as just generally supporting each other. I liked what I saw, and the idea of replicating something similar in each community. The staff were keen to help and show me the ropes and then provided me with a list of charities to send my documents to.

The excitement in me started to grow out of all proportion; I began to feel really giddy and silly, which spurred me on to produce more and more documents.

Andy Kershaw made the mistake of supplying me with contact details for all the MPs up and down the country and, by the end of the third day, all the MPs in the North of England had received copies of my ranting, along with numerous other agencies. Replies were coming in thick and fast and Connexions and South Yorkshire Police had also been in touch.

Night after night I produced my work, and each day I ran up and down to BBC Radio Sheffield with new pieces of writing ready to be mailed out.

I prided myself that I was now not only a successful business person, social campaigner and activist but also a superb communicator. Buzzing with confidence, motivation, energy and focus, everyone who I came into contact with wanted to assist me in my venture. It seemed like a miracle combination but it was also like surfing a wave; I didn't know whether I was ten feet up or ten feet below. I wondered if I had swallowed a powerful drug. I wondered if this was the kind of feeling that you get from taking speed or cocaine.

Refusing to believe that there was anything wrong with me, I ploughed on regardless for the cause. To make the vision authentic, I'd gathered together sixteen of my daughter's friends and begun to talk to them about the vision. Excited about the project they agreed to weekly meetings to discuss the plans. A few of the girls were particularly enthused and wanted to contribute work: this was the first time I'd seen the kids so enthusiastic about anything, other than getting drunk or smoking weed. I recognised it had given them a sense of purpose.

If this was going to get off the ground we needed to launch this vision properly so I approached the local primary school to ask for a venue for the meeting and reluctantly they let us have their hall for free.

With the meeting all set, all that was left to do was to decide what it was about. I had decided that it was initially going to be presented to professionals and local businesses to get them on board first. This was far 'too big' for the general public.

I couldn't stop writing; my enthusiasm was at its height. It felt like all my life I had been waiting to blossom into creativity, so setting up a project like this was to be one of my greatest achievements. But as the enthusiasm in me grew so did my skewed perceptions. I started to feel like I was on top of the world and no one could touch me; I was being driven by a higher force. I was rich, richer than anyone could ever imagine. Informing Faye of my new found wealth, which didn't (and still doesn't) exist, she naturally became over excited and started to tell all her friends in school how clever and rich her mother was and that she didn't need to do her work as she didn't need qualifications because she would be working for the project. School was getting concerned about all the twittering about the project.

Not realising it, I was actually making myself more and more vulnerable and it was becoming obvious to people, both at work and also in the community, that I was quite unwell.

I sent out an email.

The Aim

Gosh, I bet some of you are dying for me now to tell you what I think we should have some money for in Gleadless, Basegreen and Intake and how I intend to get some of these issues that I have previously raised with you SORT-ed out. I have been speaking to a lot of people recently, mostly nice people that understand that there is an urgent need for change within our society and some that do not always understand that everyone has different problems within their own lives. I have also spoken to some MPs, some shop keepers, some parents, some schools, the BBC, small cottage industries in the community and some professionals in education, health, housing, police, drugs workers, social services and the young people in my community. I have not spoken to one person over the last couple of weeks that does not think that my ideas are of some value.

I will start by telling you what my goal is and how I think it can be achieved.

I would like to achieve a project in our community that would be either built by young people and trades people in the local area that will get paid a fair wage for their services. This could either be done by using an existing building in the local area that is derelict or from scratch on a piece of land that may be available in the local area. This will be supported by local businesses by the use of their facilities and they will be paid too.

Activities will be organised and run through outreach services for disabled people and people with mental health problems and other disadvantaged groups in our community.

Open learning sessions will be delivered to adults on issues like drugs, positivity, how to start businesses, smoking cessation classes, slimming classes, keep fit classes, pilates, and yoga. So I want lots of adult education classes running alongside projects that the young people can be involved in both in the building and also around the community.

For the young people they would like a place to sit and chat, a place where they can build bridges with other young people that may have some problems and talk openly to them about that in group discussion.

They would like to have accurate, up-to-date information on what drugs are being sold in the UK, what is legal and what is not, what will kill them and what won't, what to do if they had their drinks spiked by someone else and they were scared, and who to tell if they are having problems that they do not know how to deal with.

They would also like builders, plasterers, electricians, joiners, crafts people, hairdressers, beauticians, nail technicians, aromotherapists and sports people to come to their project and show them how to make things and how to use their skills to make a living.

So, there it is. A big project thought of by a little person, supported by some other small little business people in the community and designed by another small but actually quite tall designer in Durham.

We can build this project in two ways.

With the help of several small people, some business people and some professionals can set this business up in our community with the help of charities, good, caring larger businesses like Morrison's, HSBC and B&Q.

We are also trying to get pop stars and comedians who are nice and care about people on board with this but that will take a bit of time.

The other way in which this project could work is by using government money to set it up, and although I doubt whether anyone in the government is able to give me any money for this I am always interested in having a go.

This project for us is about bringing people together in our community to try and make things better. It's about people recognising that being angry and nasty gets you nowhere in life and that nice things happen to those who work hard and treat others with respect. It's also about helping people who do not know how to be helped to make their lives better and more stable and it's about challenging those who treat people with differences better.

Kathryn

Like most mornings, the following morning had started off chaotically. I had a meeting set up with the head of a church and a meeting with the head of Sheffield Futures. I'd woken at 2am again and had been unable to get back to sleep. The alcohol I was consuming was only knocking me out for a short while, after which I would wake up feeling even worse than the day before.

I had contacted so many people over the last few weeks that I had lost track of who I had said what to.

Ash from Sheffield Futures brought a colleague to my home, a trendy-looking youth worker. They had received my email and were intrigued to know more. They looked at the room filled with bits of paper. 'You need to gather it all up and try and get it in some sort of order, people are gonna wanna know how you've set this up you know.' I felt excited that someone was validating my ideas. Maybe this was big after all. 'Record everything, record who you have spoken to, who you have met and what they have said,' he added, 'otherwise it will all get too big for you to cope with.'

The problem was that the conversations had already got muddled, everything was getting muddled and as excited as I was, I also felt as if I was drowning, drowning in brandy, drowning in life, drowning in nonsense.

They returned to their office to see what help they could

offer, leaving me in the front room, surrounded by paper, and feeling very overwhelmed.

★

The day of the meeting had arrived. In the dining hall of the local school, we had set out about a hundred chairs in four large lines facing the front. I wanted the young people all to be sitting in a line facing the audience. Time was running out and I was starting to panic, not about the speech – I had that in the bag – but about people not turning up. I'd publicised well: within a week I'd campaigned across the whole of the country. Emails and phone calls, radio phone-ins, you name it, I'd done it. I wanted the press there too so I had contacted the *Guardian*, the *Mail* and the *Observer*. I was frightened that there would be a media stampede and that they would all want an exclusive, I started to think figures for an exclusive story on the project. A few hundred would be a good figure.

Nervously, I waited in the school playground. People began to arrive, friends of mine, God I was getting excited: *five, six, seven*, I counted in my head as they passed by and began to fill up the hall. Half past seven came and went and only a few people had turned up, some from housing, some from education and a lady from the youth offending team. I felt a sick feeling in the pit of my stomach. This was my big performance and there were hardly any people here. Did no one care about the problems in society? Were people so busy getting on with their pathetic little dull lives to notice that we were all facing a crisis on a monumental scale?

Anger started to grow inside me. Prompted by a friend to move it along I took to the stage with the young people sat behind me dressed in their SORT-ed t-shirts. I felt overwhelmingly confident as I swung from one sentence to another, delivering my piece on the corrosion of the community and the government's misuse of public funds. Everyone seemed very engaged and as I passionately delivered my speech, I felt euphoric. At the end the young people rose to their feet, held hands and sang along to the Lighthouse family 'High'. And I was very high.

*

I kept trying to get an appointment with the G.P, but to no avail. Days and days went by and still no appointment. I was worried that I was now off work sick as my annual leave was over and the prospect of returning to work filled me with dread. 'Can I have an appointment to see a doctor please?' I begged each morning after a half hour wait hanging on trying to get through.

'Sorry all our appointment slots are now gone, you'll have to ring back in the morning,' the arrogant receptionist spouted down the phone. On and on it went, day after day and all the while my anger was growing, aimed at everyone, in particular Tony Blair.

The following day a friend called. 'Kathryn, this line doesn't sound right to me,' he commented. Immediately I knew. Deep within my heart, I knew that people were afraid of me, that I was the rebel, the force to be reckoned with. I had become a whistleblower. 'They' were afraid of me, the people in the government and 'they' wanted to know my every move, who I was talking to and what was I talking about. 'They' had bugged my phone, that was clear.

'You need to be careful who you are talking to, Faye,' I said as I sat her down on the sofa to try and explain this rationally. 'I think people are watching us,' I explained. I went outside to check down the path and noticed that the bin had gone. I panicked as I knew that bin day was tomorrow and that everyone else's bin was out and still full, so the bin men clearly hadn't been and I hadn't taken it anywhere. My heart raced. Where was my wheelie bin?

I had to get my bin back and, infuriated by this heinous act, I went straight to my computer and emailed the local news reporter, Andy Kershaw from BBC Radio Sheffield, people at work, previous managers, anyone that I thought would have a real and genuine interest in the fact that my wheelie bin had gone missing.

I dialled 999. This was not just an act of theft but an attempted elimination of me. Whoever stole my wheelie bin knew exactly what they were doing as they were looking for my writings, my papers on how I was going to change the world. 'I need to report a theft,' I said impatiently. 'There are some really, really important documents in that wheelie bin that could get into the hands of the wrong people,' I explained to her with a sense of urgency. Everything had become urgent and fast and if I wanted something doing I wanted it doing there and then.

'You will have to go to the local police station to file an incident report,' she explained.

Without hesitation, I jumped in my clapped out blue Nova and drove to Moorway Police Station: the wheelie bin thief had to be caught.

★

Inside of me was a mixture of anxiety and euphoria. It felt as if I had fallen into a deep trance where a golden beam of light had lifted me into another dimension.

I had the power to infect people with happiness and each day I spread my joy around my community. People seemed to be anxious of me. I walked into shops in the community and sat down at a random desk and told them to print me so many copies of this document and that document that I had on a

33

disk. Work had become increasingly nervous of me, approaching me with caution like I was bomb waiting to explode. I glowed with energy and this energy filled every room I walked into like a thousand-watt bulb.

I had also started being sick in the morning, every morning. I'd have to run to the bathroom and empty the contents of my stomach. I felt chronic anxiety but couldn't seem to let go of the idea that this was what I needed to be doing and that I now had a new purpose in life and work no longer mattered. I pushed on in pursuit of my goal, an obsession that I couldn't stop and like a merry-go-round it spun and it spun round and round so fast that I couldn't get off.

The writing kept on coming day and night and the send button would be pressed attaching my documents that had not been checked. It was straight from the heart, naive writing and a big pile of rubbish and just as the writing kept on coming, so did my public appearances. I set meetings up with as many people as I could fit into a day including local MPs, the Chief Inspector of South Yorkshire Police and the heads of the health service. In each meeting I became more and more demanding that things needed to be done in order to make our community a better place to live in.

This project was my main focus and nothing else mattered. I went to the shop to purchase some more brandy and got comfortable on the sofa. We needed some music in this venture so at 1am I picked up the phone and began to contact record companies.

My first phone call was to Chrysalis records, 'I want to speak with David Gray,' I said to a foreigner on the other end of the phone. 'It's really important that David Gray contacts me now.'

'You will have to phone back in the morning, there is no one here now,' he replied.

I replaced the receiver. I made the same phone calls to

various agencies, including the Saatchi Gallery but it was very late and no one was there. I phoned Vegas, Singapore, Mexico and Alabama racking up the best part of an £800 phone bill in one month.

The next morning I continued on my mission to contact companies and after many failed attempts to ring the Saatchi Gallery I finally got through.

'I've got a penis,' I explained to the girl on the other end of the phone. 'I think that Charles would be very interested in my nine foot penis that I have built in my garden, it's a symbol of how I feel about Tony Blair. I'm building an arse as well so that Tony Blair can shove his prick up the arse of President George Bush.' She started laughing, not at me particularly but laughing in a shocked way. 'Well I don't know how the hell people get their art into these galleries so I'm phoning you,' I exclaimed.

'Well I'm Maddy and it all sounds very interesting, errr, what's your name?' she asked.

'Kathryn, that's my name and I'm a social worker and I'm in a right muddle, I think I'm a bit unwell, I'm think I'm having errr, some sort of a breakdown I think, well actually I'm not sure whether I am having a breakdown or a break through, either way it's all good, well anyway, can you get him to contact me urgently?' I said at breakneck speed, not even coming up for breath.

'So, let me get this right, you have built a nine foot penis in your garden and you want me to ask Charles Saatchi if you can display it here, am I right?

'Yep, perfect.' I liked Maddy a lot. 'OK, well if you leave me some contact details then I will certainly pass this onto to someone,' she added. I gave her my phone number, address and email and said my goodbyes.

I was on top of the world. My head was already starting to plan the next stage of the project: *perhaps we could have an exhibition in his gallery*, I thought, *where sixteen white mannequins in a white room with the SORT-ed t-shirts on could be in a circle with different music and words playing out of each one. Each child could say a piece about what they would like to have in their community.*

I was full of an anxious combination of excitement and zest. I was fed up with living in a world of work with no sense of adventure or risk, and I had lost all spontaneity and, with that, the capacity to feel and express myself creatively. I had developed a neurotic dissatisfaction with myself. I had so much potential for energy and enthusiasm and it was suddenly spilling out like an overflowing cup of hot coffee, all over the table, all over my life but a part of me felt like I was dying and this was my chance to speak out, to achieve something good and great.

I had started to crash, suffering from compassion fatigue but as much as I knew I needed to down tools, I could not stop writing, day after day, night after night I wrote reams and reams of nonsense but it wasn't all nonsense. Deep within the piles of shite sat some golden nuggets, which I then decided to turn into a book. I was going to write a book about growing up in Gleadless, a funny book filled with tragedy, love and laughter, a book my mum would be proud of. I had made a complete fool of myself in my community so I was to now stay in my bedroom out of harm's way and concentrate on better things.

FOUR

The Ordinary House
April 20th 2004

SORT-ED WAS OLD HAT. I'd moved on, bored. As instant as
Readybrek, the idea had been abandoned and something else
was developing. Mum's seventieth birthday was on the horizon
and I wanted so much to give her something special. She
deserved it. I wanted to give her a unique gift, something she
had never had: a book written for her about her and us. What I
didn't realise was that, as quickly as I had started writing down
memories of our childhoods, dark thoughts came into my
head, thoughts and memories that I didn't want to have, didn't
want to think about and soon, what had started off as a gift to
my mother, became the opening of Pandora's box.

Book for Mother
Chapter One

It was the year that equal pay was introduced to women
in Australia, alongside Queen Victoria's own
introduction of the 'P' plate for probationary drivers.
4,000,000 people attended Woodstock, Britain was
admitted into the EEC and the age of voting was
reduced to age eighteen. The Kray twins were jailed for

thirty years and, at the age of eighteen, Bernadette Delvin became the youngest ever British MP. Inflation was a worldwide problem and the QE2 made her maiden voyage to New York.

It was also the same year that my friend Maxine was born; Maxine was always the one who liked to show her knickers to the boys when doing handstands. It was the same year that my friend Louise was born too, who by the way still has a copy of my Girls annual stashed away on her top shelf and to this day refuses to return it. 1969 was a great year for me as I was born.

There are three of us; I am the runt of the litter. There were meant to be five but Mum told me my sister, Judith, the second born child had sadly died and that I was a twin. My twin had died in the womb and my mum told me that when my twin died, she didn't know she was still pregnant with me. 'None of that medical equipment in them days, you know,' she said. So I was a miracle baby I guess, a baby that no one knew was there right up until the big push. My big sister, Valerie, was eight at the time of my arrival and my older brother, Nicholas, two and a half. He hated me and I hated him, a typical 1970's brother and sister relationship. He had a farm and I had a doll, I wanted his farm and he didn't want my doll. Boys always seem to have the bestest toys. I was never allowed near them and, if I dared, he would pin me down and spit on my face. On more than one occasion he drew snot on my Starsky and Hutch poster, and he spent most days generally making my life a misery. 'Skilly boy' that's what he called himself; I couldn't see anything 'Skilly' about him.

Our house was magical. There were always buttons, silks and ribbons to touch and feel, wool to knit with and material to stitch with. You could make anything you wanted to in our house. We had clay to play with that mum would bring home from night school and occasionally, as a real treat, she would borrow the potter's wheel. Each night, when we lay in our beds, we could hear a rumbling noise downstairs: Mum on her sewing machine. Mum was creative; she could make anything out of anything. One day you could have a dress, one that you may have quite liked; the next day you could have a brand new trouser suit that used to be your dress.

All you had to do was choose a pattern and voila! it was made. Like magic, Mum would transform, create and mend. She once made me this giant size green boiler suit with an elastic waist out of shiny green waxed cotton; I wanted to look like Olivia Newton John, but ended up looking more like a cross between the Incredible Hulk and the Jolly Green Giant.

However, it didn't deter me from wearing it to the 1980 Junior Star disco at Stars night club, the highlight of my life where I coined my first kiss with the caretaker's son whose breath smelled like a pig's bottom.

I had a big family with lots of cousins, aunts and uncles, some of whom arrived on a plane at Christmas from Chicago and brought unusual things like M&Ms and popcorn. More aunts and uncles came from India and brought silks and jewellery in parcels with our names on labels. Christmas was a great time when we all got together to take pictures. We took lots of pictures. The slide show came out every Christmas and we all sat in amazement at the videos and pictures of ourselves when we were babies.

We were good kids, two generations of Girls and

Boys Brigaders. We marched everywhere: the Lord Mayor's Parade, the Easter parade and the Whitsun tide parade. We marched anywhere and everywhere.

We had our weekend routines: Saturdays were for seeing Granny L, and Sundays were for seeing Granny B. Granny L lived in a high rise flat at Claywood, on floor seven. Our cousins would meet us there and we would play in the lifts and throw rubbish down the chute to hear it drop to the ground, counting how many seconds it took to land. Granny L did the best meat and potato pie in the whole world, always with a rose petal and leaves on top. I always got the rose. We drank Tizer from the pop man and played with the maggots he used to warm up on his tongue that would wiggle in our hands. Granny L had blue and pink big plastic rings in her jewellery box and she had wigs and a dressing up box. They smelt disgusting.

Granny L was a bread and dripping kind of person, she was born and raised on Low Street, which got bombed in the war. It was the only house out of a row of fifteen that was left standing, a miracle. She was down to earth and special. No airs and graces, kind and wonderful. She had the biggest boobs you have ever seen. They expanded and deflated as she snored her way through her sleep. We slept five in a bed when we all stayed at Granny L's, the two boys on one side of granny and me and my cousin on the other side. It was like being on a wave machine, up and down to Granny's snoring we went until we fell into a deep slumber.

At Granny B's house you were met with the same love and kindness. She had different interesting things, dressing up boxes, pantries full of odd knick-knacks. We played in her courtyard and walked for miles in Jilly Woods in Totley where she lived. We would meet up with our other set of cousins and laugh and play until it was time to catch the 97 bus home.

I loved our road and I loved our lives: on the surface, it was the idyllic childhood. Our road was special and safe. A cul-de-sac where everyone seemed like they had lived there forever. It was as if they had been specially selected to make our lives perfect. We all went to the same school; we all shopped at the same shop and all went to the same church. This was suburbia; this was middle England.

★

People around me didn't understand what was happening and neither did I. The world had sped up and I was trying as hard as I could to keep up with the hundred mile an hour pace I was now operating at.

I tried hard to search for nice things that had happened in my childhood but was finding it increasingly difficult. I wanted this to be a nice book, something she could look at and feel proud of. All the memories, the good times we had had, they were all there but something darker and more sinister was getting in the way. I thought about all the talent contests that I had entered as a child: a bluebell fairy, Old Mother Hubbard, a Jack-in-a-box, the list was endless. All of which seemed to be clouded by the terrors that haunted my mind, visions of episodes of frightening scenes that had played out alongside all the wonderfulness of my childhood. Two contradictory and conflicting lives in one house.

Thoughts came thick and fast, whirling, spinning, nipping, kicking and punching as I vomited the kaleidoscope of painful memories over the page. Something rumbling inside me, like stomach cramps following an overindulgent night of several bottles of wine and curry, brewing, cramping, waiting for the inevitable explosion. But first was the wretchedness that engulfed me in the vain attempt to remind me to never, ever drink again. Not for a few hours at least.

The brewing cyclone of diarrhoea about to spew out all over the place was the story of my life, my childhood. The deepest, darkest memories etched into each corner of my mind that, for many years, had been wobbling around anaesthetised and covered up by far too much booze, endorphins and sleep deprivation had come staggering blindly to the surface. They bashed wildly from the depths of my temporal lobe, via the cerebrum and out through the hand that was holding the pen.

Looking from the outside, our house on Heatherfield Road was just an ordinary house; a detached house with an apex roof, three windows and a door. The garden was always in bloom and the window frames were painted every two years. It was a simple era where toys and puzzles came in cereal packets, Golliwogs weren't political, and we marvelled over scientific calculators. Our world was more complex, and it was a world where – for me – being small equalled powerlessness.

The dichotomy of my childhood in the sixties and seventies had had a profound effect on my life and it was no one's fault.

Mum and Dad had worked hard and had done fairly well for themselves. They had moved up the social mobility ladder by buying the three-bed detached house, which was, at the time, a new build. Mum was a nurse in A&E at the Children's Hospital and Dad was an accountant who, before he got sick, worked for Arthur Laddells, a steel stockholder in Sheffield. When he got sick, Arthur Laddells were quick to dispose of Dad, packing him off with a large box of red apples.

Dad was ill, very ill. Nothing was his fault and that was the problem. There was no one to blame. I never really knew

Dad, or 'him', as I used to refer to him. 'He was a lovely man your dad,' everyone was always keen to remind me of what life was like before the sickness struck. He didn't seem that lovely to me and all I knew was what I knew. The illness had savagely turned him into someone entirely different to the person Mum had married: it had altered his personality, affected his moods and his temperament. Granny L had told me he was sick because he had suffered meningitis when he was little and that had caused him to have swelling on his brain in later life. I thought that he had fallen off a ladder when I was five and cracked his head on the concrete. Mum had told me that Dad had what was called a lot of 'grand mal seizures'.

One sunny day I was playing in my friend's front garden with our fairies. We would make them houses out of lolly pop sticks and feed them bread dipped in orange juice. Neighbours began to frantically run up the road to our house; then came an ambulance. Mum was at work. Aunty Nora came round from next door and took me to hers. As I walked out onto the street Dad was being carried off on a stretcher, his head covered in blood. Aunty Nora pulled me close to her so that my head was in her apron and then she took me inside her house. I don't really know what happened after that but I knew that things changed. The atmosphere changed from being happy and safe to being tense and frightening. Mum would always be stressed and cross, she never seemed happy again.

As the years progressed dad got worse and worse and so did the tension in the house. His violent fits became the norm and had a certain unpredictable predictability to them. We learned to spot the signs. To the untrained eye you wouldn't even notice the onset. First came the slavering, sometimes his eyes would roll back. He'd do silly things like pour the whole salt pot onto his dinner in a big snow mountain or phone someone up and tell them he was divorcing Mum because she was voting Conservative. His upset would have been justified if it was true, but of course it wasn't.

He wasn't lying, not as you or I understand lying, he didn't know what he was doing. He'd wet himself and over time his fits made his behaviour violent and difficult to control. The front room had become a minefield and he was the bomb waiting to go off. You constantly feared that something would trigger it. As his illness progressed, so did his frustration with it. Mum was trying to cope with three children, a disabled husband, a full-time job to pay the bills – there was no Disability Living Allowance in those days – and her own sanity. His despair at both the lack of input he was having in the family home, coupled with his decreasing inability to self-care, gave rise to a new and scarier situation.

Dad was not only violent when he was 'fitting'; he had become aggressive when he wasn't. Mum had little time to empower him and enable him to do things for himself, which, in turn, frustrated him even more. It took Dad a long time just to walk from one end of the room to the other and for Mum, who needed to operate at high speed, just to keep on top of everyone's needs and demands, the house probably seemed more like a prison than a family home.

Valerie didn't like Dad at all and she made it clear. She was really brave, much braver than me but she was also an antagonist. She provoked situations, sometimes unnecessarily, in the knowledge that someone would get hurt. One day, I was sitting with Dad in the front room; the room was long and open plan with a dining table to the rear and a front part of the house being used as a living space. I sat peacefully on the floor sewing dolls' clothing. My sewing box contained all sorts of bits and pieces, carefully collected from scraps Mum was throwing out: buttons, wool, ribbons and satins, all with a purpose and all so important.

It was the late seventies and ankle chains were the rave.

Valerie was at the cutting edge of fashion. She was fashionable and assertive, the two qualities I didn't have, but at the age of six you don't tend to have much.

Valerie walked into the room wearing an ankle chain. 'Take that off now,' Dad demanded as she strutted across the room towards the mirror, 'you look like a common prostitute,' he spattered at her.

Before I knew what was happening, an argument broke out and she moved so that she stood behind me, facing the wall whilst continuing to put her make up on in the mirror. 'I'm not taking it off,' she said tersely.

This act of defiance infuriated him even more, 'Don't you dare back chat me young lady,' he said as he tried to steady himself in the upright position holding onto his tripod walking stick. They both stood facing each other, towering above me, my pins, needles, buttons and ribbons, her with her mascara in her hand and him with his tripod. I was frozen. He raised his hand to swipe her clean across the face, she pushed his arm out of the way and he staggered backwards. Hands over my head, I tried to protect myself from the attack. He composed himself then in one swift move he lifted his tripod and pinned her face neatly to the wall, like a wasp being captured in a glass jar to either be released outside or suffer the fate of death by suffocation.

'You're nothing but a common prostitute!' he shouted again. I had no idea what a prostitute was, I'd never heard the word. She pushed hard and he quickly lost balance, falling sideways. I watched in slow motion, silently, as the seventeen-stone man fell, missed me by millimetres, and cracked the side of his head directly onto the melamine coffee table. Blood splattered on my face, my dolly and my ribbons, my beautiful blue ribbons.

Mum was a nurse and she mended everyone. Children were brought from far and wide for my mum's healing touch.

She tended to cuts, grazes, stomach upsets and broken bones. She mended everyone but she couldn't mend 'him'.

Eventually, Valerie couldn't take anymore and, after she had finished art school she left home. 'I'm getting the hell out of here and I'm going as far away as I possibly can,' she snapped at me one day. I felt abandoned. She was my protector and her leaving made me feel so much more vulnerable. I feared for our safety. Each night when we went to bed I would try and stay awake, waiting for him to start fitting, to launch his assaults on Mum. I would try all sorts of things to keep myself awake, such as pinching myself with a comb or eating, and eating became my sedative of choice. I'd wake in the morning to find a bucket at the top of the stairs and the 'spoon'. The 'spoon' was a symbol of a problematic night. A large dessert spoon with plaster wrapped round the handle. Mum used it to push it into his mouth when he fitted to stop him swallowing his tongue. I wished, night after night, that she would just let him choke, let him end his own misery and our suffering.

Finally, when I was about twelve, Mum made the decision that Dad could no longer live with us. With this news I felt exhilarated. My work at school improved and I started to be a bit happier until I found out that he would be coming home at weekends. When all, the kids in school were buzzing about having the weekend off, I would have a sick feeling in the pit of my stomach, knowing that we would have an angrier-than-ever father coming home. He hated it in Skye Edge residential home and he hated Mum for putting him there. Each Sunday afternoon, Mum would begin the process of packing him up for his return. This was a dangerous time, when he would often lash out at her as he felt he was being turfed out of his home, but Mum had made this decision based on our safety not his.

Eventually, I got my wish when, five minutes into my

thirteenth birthday in 1982, the same year that ABC released their debut album, *Lexicon of Love,* my dad died. At 12.05am our phone rang. It was an unusual time for the phone to ring. Mum went downstairs and I followed her. I stood outside in the hall listening while she took the call. I could tell by her voice it was bad news and my fear was that it was my Granny B that had died. I entered the room to find Mum sitting there shaking. 'It's your dad, he's dead.' The phone was still in her hand so I replaced it onto the receiver. Her face was as white as a sheet.

I felt shocked. Shocked that this was what I had prayed for so many years and it had finally happened. I couldn't understand how he could have died. He didn't have a physical illness that was life-threatening. On that night, my birthday night, I felt like we had all been released, like we had been freed from a horrendous situation. I would never have thought that our experiences could have done so much damage to our relationships with each other but it did.

The ordinary looking house still stands in the ordinary street, that house with a family with not so ordinary problems.

I thought about that birthday as I drank more brandy. I wondered whether Dad dying on my birthday was a sign, a sign to say that it was my fault or that he didn't like me and I would be haunted by him forever. I was developing tolerance to brandy; I needed to drink more and more in order for it to have the anaesthetising effect that I needed. I had always been a wine drinker but for some reason felt that I needed something stronger. I began driving to different shops, developing a circuit, avoiding suspicions from the wider community, the nosey bastards with little else to do than gossip. I loved my community but I hated it as well. I didn't fit in; we didn't fit in. Single parent, white middle-class suburbia.

I can't quite remember what was happening in my world before I entered complete 'mentaldom'. I knew it I was different and I knew I had felt unwell for many years but before I had always managed to hold it together despite not sleeping. Now it seemed that everything was coming apart at the seams faster than I had chance to gather it all up and put it all back together. Food shopping had gone out of the window. Faye was spending more and more time away from the house and I had no idea what she was getting up to and I wasn't sure I wanted to know. We had entered into a crazy zone.

I realised at some point, though, that I had been in my room for some time. If I had to leave the house I would do so speedily so I could get back as quickly as possible. I was becoming a recluse. I was finding it harder and harder to care for myself and my daughter, and impossible to care for the cat as I was struggling to meet my own personal needs.

Flitting from thought to thought, I was onto the next chapter in the book for my mum. I felt angry inside but didn't understand why. I tried to think and remember the nice times that I had had growing up, hanging around with my friends.

Book for Mother
Chapter Two

One-fouring it!

'One four for a copy, one four for a copy,' we would say to attract blokes on my mate Louise's CB radio in her back bedroom.

'Wanna eyeball,' they'd reply.

We knew it was dangerous, so we would arrange to meet lads round the corner of Woods shop on Ridgeway Road. We'd laugh at them, the ugly boys, who arrived one after the other after chatting to us on the radio in Louise's bedroom. They would come looking bewildered and confused. We would hide and giggle.

We never smoked or drank; we didn't steal or swear, we had better things to do with our time like collecting and examining stick insects in our garage, doing catamaran's on skateboards from the top of the road to the bottom, six on top, and four on the bottom. We tied fishing wire to old wallets and watched as people went to pick them up only to pull it away. We tied all the door handles together on the road with string but best of all Louise and me spent hours 'one-fouring it' in her bedroom.

★

My thought process had become obscured and I started to act out irrational behaviours like putting the mincemeat in the washing machine on a hot wash. I put eggs in my car radiator and ironed a frozen chicken but one thing that remained constant was my writing. I kept on writing. My computer had become my sanctuary; I felt safe in my room with my computer but had no idea what was going to happen next.

FIVE

Aligning to Zero
April 14th 2004

I MADE MY FINAL VISIT to the BBC, feeling very wobbly indeed, knowing that I was really poorly and that my attentions were now firmly centred on writing a book. As it was now obvious that I was a total nut job, Mr Kershaw seemed relieved that I had come to this conclusion myself. Suffering exhaustion from my overbearing personality and the 'need for speed', he signposted me to the next set of unsuspecting victims, the *INKY* team.

INKY is a local writing magazine that holds a drop-in for new writers at the library each Wednesday evening and I was keen to swing by. Their ethos is that anyone can, and should, write.

Perfect, I thought to myself, these were exactly the people that I needed in my life. Having written nearly twenty chapters, I thought I would take a sample to them of what I had been working on. When I say twenty chapters, some of the chapters didn't have very much in them, in fact some of them only had one word. It was more like a compendium of meaningless twaddle than a book, but I didn't care because to me it was 'my story', my life's work and I knew I was a genius. I knew it would be a best seller and that we were finally going to be financially stable. If the SORT-ed project wasn't a goer then the most famous book in the world was.

Book for Mother
Chapter Nineteen

Mablethorpe to Mauritius

> The bestest place to be in the whole wide world would be in a little hut near the seaside or a lake somewhere far away with baroque, panpipes for lovers, Johnny Cash and a very lovely man friend to have lots of good sex and conversations about complete nothingness. Anywhere will do from Mablethorpe to Mauritius.

Like a child in urgent need of instant gratification I rushed to the library. Making sure I had the right time and place, I scanned and rescanned the newsletter. (This behaviour of hurrying to get feedback was a theme in my behaviour that ran throughout the episode, at least until the bad bits started.) I was writing stuff and sending it to people to get immediate reaction. Having approval and positive feedback, especially from work, was, like for most people stuck in the dreary humdrum of normality, something I had been lacking.

I was so excited about meeting the guy from *INKY*, Matt Blonc. He was a star in the writing world, having published over twenty-eight books, poems and little pamphlets. I wanted him to have a look at my book and tell me if I had a chance of getting it published: if anyone was the guy, he was. I had visions of him wanting to work on it in collaboration with me, visions of him getting me on television. I dreamed of us sitting on the sofa with Richard and Judy and then popping in to do a live broadcast with Sharon Osbourne, followed by a flight to the States to be on Oprah Winfrey. I was certain he was going to be impressed.

Like a child queuing at the tuck shop, I waited in eager anticipation whilst he mulled over the pages of my writing. He looked over the first couple of pages, skim reading it.

'What do you think?' I asked.

'Well, you have got something here,' he said as he continued to read on, flicking through to see if there was more than one word or one paragraph on some of the sheets. 'When you are writing,' he said, 'just simply look around the room that you are sat in, you don't need any more than what is around you,' he added.

Was that it? Was that all I was going to get? I felt disappointed. This enormous build up and then, 'all I need to write a book is to look in the space that I am in at the time?' I repeated back.

'Yes, that's all you need, to get you started at least.'

So really what he was saying was, 'Look Kathryn, you have a long, long way to go yet.' I didn't like that.

He repeated, 'Everything you need is right with you.'

As philosophical as all this was and, despite my parade being pissed upon, I thought that he may have got a point. For it was true that the first part of this book had indeed been nicked from an old diary of historical events that had simply been laying on my book shelf, so perhaps I did have it all in my bedroom, to hand.

I informed Matt that I was really unwell, that I had a slight fever and was feeling a touch stressed. I was afraid to use the word mental. My head was about to explode. I moved away from the desk pretending to be searching for a book. My whole physical being felt so fragile, like an old woman. I was overdrawn on all accounts. He had a kind nature and could see that it was all a bit 'mental'. He gave me some valuable writing tips and I stepped aside for others to show him their work.

That evening, the writing continued. Sleep had still not kicked in; I was more alert than ever. I had forgotten how to sleep and sleeping also brought with it the fear of dying: if I slept I may never wake up. I had exhausted all natural remedies and bottles and bottles of herbal remedies filled my drawer – none of them effective.

As I wrote, I had a need to send it to people so that they could see what I was writing. Email after email went, to family and friends, seeking recognition for my marvellous efforts. Nothing I sent had been proofread, just written and sent. No checking, no monitoring, for I was a writer now, I didn't need to check things, proofread or edit anything. I was a brilliant writer and this was a masterpiece, my 'epic' novel which was on a par with *War and Peace*, having no fewer than ninety-two chapters. It mattered not that the chapters weren't in order or that some of the chapters only had one word or even one letter written on them, there were ninety-two and counting them mattered.

I considered whether a boyfriend would help to ease my angst but then quickly decided against it as life was complicated. I did want love, though; love that required no effort on my part and total adoration of me on the part of 'the lover'. A boyfriend that didn't demand much and someone who I rarely had to see or engage with, as I was so busy and all. A 'Tamagotchi boyfriend' would be perfect. However, my 'Tamagotchi boyfriend' wasn't going to be able to share the most worrying aspect of my existence, the increasing costs of general day-to-day living, which was what I also needed help with.

I'd had boyfriends, all nice but just not quite 'it'. Some had landed on my doorstep to be fixed, most with some sort of baggage. They had a pattern, a theme that ran throughout; they all eventually wanted looking after and the prospect of that did not enthuse me. Starting off as exciting, loving, daring, dangerous and spontaneous, then changing overnight, like the wind, they'd transform into sofa sluts, mummy's boys, boring, gluttonous slobs.

As an independent woman of the '90s, I demanded more from life. I wanted fun, love, passion and – not least – someone who would share the bills. I had loads of love to give but no one to aim it at. It felt immense, bursting at the seams, crippling my solar plexus. However, I kept on shooting little arrows into the most ill-chosen of places. That night, I wrote more. This time, the writings were becoming inappropriate.

E-mail sent to Andy and Matt:

'Look at me, I'm as helpless as a dog stuck up a tree,
Never knowing my right foot from left
My fingers from my glove, I'm steamy and so much in love
You can say that you're just teasing me
can't you see I'm helplessly lost, that's why I want to be near you.
must I wander throughout this wonderland on my own,
this music I know I get steamy and so much in love'.

God only knows where I had got this from, I didn't care. I knew it was wrong, so very wrong but it didn't stop me, I didn't want to stop it. There didn't seem to be a connection between the send button on the PC and the outside world, as if everything I wrote just ended up on a big fluffy cloud, the cloud of 'bonkerdom'. As if no one real would ever read it and I was immune. As if all the people outside of my front door were only there for me and I was part of a constructed reality, like in *The Truman Show*, untouchable and unstoppable, for everything I did was being enjoyed by the millions of people looking at everything I did, every minute of every day. The uncontrollable, consequence-free existence that I was living was fun but also had a dark side.

My moods were swinging from pillar to post. I kept on

writing silly emails and sending them, I couldn't help myself; the fingers, the brain and the send button continued to be in some random connected fashion. I sent angry letters and complaints to companies that had failed to deliver both goods and services that I needed. Emails went to anyone who may have upset me: politicians, large global consumerist outfits and international conglomerates were all popular targets. Capitalism was sucking the life out of society, draining our communities of cohesion and personality, and I wasn't standing for it, not any of it.

As the rich got richer, the poor and needy got left out in the cold, things were getting worse and, when the morning arrived, so did the realisation of what I had done the night before, bringing with it a cloud of despair which made me hate myself. Not able to look at what I had sent the previous night I ploughed on regardless. The more I did it, the more despair I felt, but still it continued.

Normal sounds became intense and penetrating: the cat clawing at the wooden bed, the sound of the wheelie bins being taken down people's drives, the chattering of the kids coming to and from school. In a similar way, music became intense, powerful and concentrated. All-pervading. I indulged myself in the words, the lullabies and the powerful crescendos. I always loved a good crescendo. Like an orgasm after fabulous sex, I would come to my final resting place, back where I started – at my desk, in my room with my brandy and my computer.

I fretted that, on programmes like *Extreme Makeover*, they would fail to complete the house in time or that the wife would not like the new wallpaper or carpets. Sitting on the edge of the sofa, biting my chewed-to-the-bone nails, I rocked from side-to-side in complete despair. Emotions ran high, too, when Dennis revealed to Sharon his love for her and Den and Dennis went head to head in the Queen Vic in *Eastenders*.

The news filled me with deep dread and obsessive, depressive thoughts that we were all going to die, with the constant fear of another terrorist attack like 9/11.

I felt so very angry but wasn't sure why. Angry at a world that didn't care what happened to vulnerable children and people; angry at politicians that no matter who was voted in, they were all in bed with capitalism, personal and corporate greed. I worried about the Middle East and I worried about Third World debt. I was angry but paralysed to act, to help to sort it out, to shout about it effectively and coherently, a useless person no one who couldn't do anything right. I had tried to save the world and had failed miserably and so, for now, I would sit and write my book and try as hard as I could to be quiet.

I couldn't remember how long I had been like this for, days, months, years? It had crossed my mind that I had always been like this which was a scary thought.

Flowers arrived that morning after I had made a phone call to my friend Andrea. Andrea and I had worked together for over a year and had a high level of professional respect for each other. Andrea knew that I must have been ill to have contacted her.

'Andrea, I think that I'm having a nervous breakdown, I need help and I don't know what to do. I'm scared, Andrea, it's like my whole world's coming crashing down on me. I can't stop thinking about child abuse and all the cases that I've dealt with over the last few years.'

Andrea was both supportive and empathetic. We talked for a while about the stresses of the role we were both consumed by, the struggles that she had encountered in her early years as a social worker and how she, with a lot of support, had learned to switch off, shut down from it emotionally. I needed that, someone to talk open and honestly about how things had become impossible to bear. In the savage role we played, sympathetic ears were hard to come by. Signs of weakness stood out and good, solid reputations were all important.

It was clear that work had become too much, was taking its toll on my state of well being. I had a feeling that I would never be able to return to child protection work but didn't want to accept it. I didn't know what else I could do, what else I was good at. I was good at people, working with difficult situations, and solving problems. It wasn't the time to be looking for new jobs or a total change in career, and the mere thought of having to attend interviews scared me.

Social work was much harder than anyone could imagine, more emotionally draining and complex than anything I had ever done before. The Jack of all trades, the master of none. Support was sketchy. It wasn't that you personally made decisions about people's lives, but decisions were based upon your reporting of a situation, and each worker was different in their value judgements of what makes 'good enough' parenting, what is acceptable and what is not and some were more switched on to that than others. The buck stopped with you and that was a huge burden to carry.

Many of the workers I knew were taking pills for depression. It was a career that was all consuming. Its frantic pace meant that there was no time in between to recover emotionally from the trauma each case would bring. Layers of trauma had built up in me and I had no release, no one to talk to or to share anxieties with and I had become increasingly paranoid that if I were to discuss my situation with anyone it would be to my own detriment.

So I lied. I covered up what was happening by becoming even more efficient, taking on more and more cases on to show I was coping when, inside, I was dead. I was a wreck. Inside, I was emotionally overdrawn on all accounts but the writing continued.

Burn Baby Burn

Drew had met some interesting people along her travels, one of which was Tara Clara Pumpkinson. Tara Clara had just graduated from university and had gained a rather sexy degree in Law. Upon deciding that her future should be more concerned with helping others, Tara had undertaken a Diploma Course to gain her adequate qualifications to practise as a social worker.

She walked like a gazelle: her long legs and short skirt left nothing to the imagination. Her all-over body mist glow tan shone in the summer sun, which complemented her highlights perfectly. Her long, curly talons were pristinely painted in red and her botoxed lips looked like large marshmallows.

'Where do you go to have your bikini line waxed?' she enquired as she put her key into the car door of her open top silver Audi, haphazardly parked cockeyed on the kerb, narrowly missing the disabled space, but making it impossible for three cars to park. 'I don't really have anywhere special,' Drew replied, embarrassed. Her temperature rose as she felt naked, for all and sundry may be at this moment staring at the pubic hairs that she had failed to shave, clip or wax for the last year.

Drew did not realise that you could have hair removed from your private parts by someone else. Who on earth would want to do a job like that?

'I think you had better not risk having your sun roof down if we are going to Canklock.' Canklock was one of the worst areas that North East Team covered. The kind of area that you drive through at 100 miles an hour just to avoid having your wheel trims nicked.

'Shall we do your visit first or mine?' Before Drew had time to answer or do any kind of risk assessment of the two cases Tara Clara said, 'Alright we'll do mine and then it's over with isn't it, you'll love this house, it's a f**cking state, dog shit and kids everywhere, I thought I'd better visit as her new baby looked a bit ill last month and the education welfare officer has contacted me again, the other kids haven't been going to school, don't know what's happening there, ah well let's check it out.'

As we pulled up, several kids were hanging around outside. There was a strong smell of weed and the front door was wide open.

'Is that you Tara,' a muffled voice shouted, 'one minute, stay there don't come in yet I'm just cooking and I've f**kin made a bit of a f**king mess. Give me ten minutes,' the voice said.

'Eh up Johnny, what you doing here, should you not be in school?' Drew had spotted one of her clients within the group.

'Let me have a look at your face darling,' she asked, 'What's happened Johnny? Who's hit you sweetheart?'

Ah f**k off, think I'm tellin' you, you'll f**king put me in that shit hole kids home again, so why don't you just f**k off and pick on some other poor bastard.'

'What you been taking my love?' Drew asked. Johnny had a large red rash around his mouth with open sores.

'What part of f**k off you don't you understand you silly bitch, Mum says you're a f**king interfering f**king bitch and to stay away from our house from now on.'

'You know I can't do that darling, I have a duty to make sure that you and your brother and sisters are safe and being looked after.'

'Yeah right, what do you f**kin know about owt?'

'Tell your mother I will be calling on her shortly and that you better be in school tomorrow or I shall be picking you up myself. If you don't go to school you're mum will be fined and you wont have any chances of a future Johnny.'

'So f**king what,' he replied and then he was off. 'F**king social workers!' Johnny shouted down the path, 'Only come if you're gonna f**king bring some f**king money you bitch.'

'Yeah, whatever, Johnny. Remember school,' Drew replied.

The house was damp and sockets hung from the walls. A pile of faeces was in the corner of the kitchen, human faeces. Pieces of worn carpet covered the floor, where there was no carpet, there was cardboard. Cockroaches scurried around the kitchen.

'You said you were gonna tell me when you were f**king calling, you know I hate this f**king unannounced visiting shit.'

Drew stepped in, 'We have a duty to visit unannounced during the time that the case is open to social services, Ms Herring, especially when there are concerns.'

'F**king concerns, what concerns, come on then f**king clever bitch, what f**king concerns,' Ms Herring splurted as she lay on the living room floor counting her valium. 'One two three four five, once I caught a fish a live.'

The stench in the house was getting too much as they both wretched, 'Where's the baby?'

'Up the f**king stairs, you wankers, where do you f**king think? F**king sleeping.'

Baby was in the corner of the room, laid in a Moses basket. Half the side had been chewed off by the local Alsatian. It was having convulsions. 'It looks a bit ill,' Tara commented.

Gunk spewed from its gob, 'It's f**king fine, now piss off.'

'I don't really do babies,' Tara said to Ms Herring, who was now laid out on some blankets in the other corner of the room pumping some nasty shit into her veins.

'Tap, tap, tap, ah that's better,' she said in a dull voice.

*

A few hours later, more flowers appeared at my door and I was overwhelmed. Another spring had gone off in my head, the tears came like a waterfall of emotion, as waves upon waves of deep pain and sorrow hit me. My stomach in knots, I needed to get to the bedroom. I crawled on my hands and knees like a wounded soldier, shot in the belly. I managed to make my way up to my room, closing the door behind me. Sitting at my desk, rocking back and forth, tears and snot dripping onto the sheets of paper that covered the keyboard. I opened my CD box and flicked through in a desperate attempt to find something to calm me down. Waves of nausea drifted over me; 'I'm dying, I'm dying!' I cried out.

This wasn't the first time I had experienced this 'thing' that was happening to me. I recalled going through something similar to this when I was at university some seven years earlier. I remembered those feelings, that dreadful second year when I had felt the same way and tried to remember that, after some months, it had passed and normal life had resumed.

I wondered what I had done to get through it. What mechanisms had I used? I knew exactly what the answers were but didn't want to accept them, for it would mean energy and commitment to the healing process; I was not strong enough to do this again. Too much energy was needed to dry out, to go through the raw, sleepless nights, to eventually come to the still point where I had been 'aligned to zero', reset, and ready to take on the world again. The alcohol was keeping me up and I didn't even know if this time I wanted to come down.

In a weird way, this was fun and exciting, like I was breaking out from societal norms and living the unexpected, but I knew the price was heavy. It had taken too much personal energy to get through, far too much. It had never had a name and I had never understood 'it', for it was just 'it': a crisis, an almighty surge of anxiety, a period of intensity. I couldn't keep this going for months, not like this. I was all too aware that I would never survive another period of sickness like last time. My body just wouldn't take it. I was getting older and the last episode had taken its toll on my health. My heart felt weaker and my lungs were struggling.

I tried calling the doctors; the line was busy. A few moments later I redialled, only to be greeted by an aggressive receptionist. 'I'm ill and I need to see a doctor urgently,' I explained.

'What's the problem?' the receptionist asked.

'Why do you have to know what the fucking problem is?' I shouted down the phone. 'My leg fell off in my sleep and my husband has run off with a crack cocaine dealer and my daughter is pregnant to an illegal immigrant, is that OK for you? I'm ill and that's all you need to know, now can I have an appointment or not?' I continued.

There is a fine line with doctors' receptionists; they think they are God's gatekeeper.

'You'll have to ring back in the morning and see if there are any appointments,' then she put the phone down before I could say anymore. I knew she was lying and just didn't like my tone but I needed help, not people making life harder.

I picked up the phone and called my manager. I needed her to know how sick I was, the stress of being off work and what they might think of me at work was getting to me and making me feel more poorly.

'She's in a meeting at the moment, shall I get her to call you back?' the receptionist said.

'Yes, yes quickly I need her.' I kneeled on the floor clutching my stomach, sobbing, *please God please what is happening to me?*

The phone rang about an hour later.

'Anita, I think I'm having a breakdown, I'm so ill, I can hardly move. I'm angry, angry at everyone.'

She spent half an hour on the phone with me, reassuring me that everything was going to be alright and stressing to me that I was a strong person who could get through this, which helped enormously. I didn't really know her that well, I'd only been on the team in Sheffield for a short time but I knew I trusted her, she was the kind of person who you know walks around with a lot of other people's information in her head. I respected her.

Feelings of rage welled within the pit of my stomach. Images of my dad assaulting my mother rushed through my head, thoughts of families that I had worked with, children that I had removed into foster care following chronic abuse and neglect. I curled up in a ball in the corner of my room.

Book for Mother
Chapter Five

Fuck Freud

I didn't think that he had had penetrative sex with her but I needed to be sure, it was procedure with a disclosure like that. I think it was the pants and discharge that the foster carer had told me about and shown me. Oh yes, and the doll, when little poppet had pointed to its genital areas. I think I did the right thing, well I know I did. It was so clinical in that room, thank goodness the foster carer came along.

I did not really understand internal examinations on children that young, they said it was normal. Normal for who? I thought, it was not normal for me. They failed to teach me about these things at university you see, it was all methods and theories and skills and Freud, Fuck Freud. He knows nowt about real life.

★

During the phone conversation with my manager, I agreed to an appointment with an emergency psychiatric nurse. She also agreed to put me in touch with TCP, an Employee Assistance Programme sub-contracted to them by Sheffield City Council to counsel staff in crisis.

I contacted them immediately.

Having been assessed by the intake worker, I was put through to a man with a rather dreamy voice. 'Hello, my name is Barry, how can I help?' I knew in that instance that Barry and I connected.

'I'm not very well Barry and I think I am going to lose my job because I can't seem to behave myself,' I sobbed down the phone. We chatted for a while and I felt calmer for having had the conversation. I didn't want him to leave me as I knew that he understood me fully.

'Don't forget we are here day and night if you need to talk to someone,' Barry added as he began drawing the conversation to a close. 'But who shall I ask for when I phone again Barry, I don't even know your surname.'

'It's Barry, Barry White,' he concluded.

'As in the singer,' I said laughing at the idea of this man with his soft, lullaby, dreamy voice was in fact called Barry White.

★

Case Notes 1

Client in tears, says that she is having a breakdown and is very scared. She does not want her daughter to see her like this and she needs to get her out of the way to school this morning.

★

I spoke to Barry several times over the course of the next few days. He was lovely. He knew that a few phone calls weren't going to fix me and he was keen for someone in the local area to have a chat with me and carry out an assessment. Barry worked in Oxford, a place I had always wanted to go to.

Barry gave me the address of a woman who lived about thirty miles away but this wasn't much use, given the state I was in; I could hardly walk, never mind drive anywhere.

Reluctantly, I drove there.

I was taken into the front room in her own house, a sparsely furnished room with white walls. I tried to explain what was happening now and what had happened over the last few weeks but the words kept getting muddled. I didn't know how much sense I was making. I got an hour with her which wasn't much, given that it had taken her over twenty minutes to do some paperwork and go over the rules. It had been a long way to drive in such a state just for relatively short talking time. I didn't want to go back and it was clear she didn't want me back. She said I was 'too unwell' for her and that I needed professional help.

I thought to myself, *I thought that's what you flippin' were*, but clearly not.

She thought I needed to see a psychiatrist. I left and that was that. I phoned Barry.

Barry was encouraging; he listened to me carefully, trying to pick out information from the mess I was spewing out at him down the phone.

'What are you scared of, Kathryn?' he asked. His direct approach surprised me; it was a question which I didn't know the answer to.

'I don't know, Barry. The world feels like it is caving in, like the clouds are going to fall from the sky, if not that then a plane will land on my home and kill us or I will just keel over and die suddenly, a heart attack probably,' I said tearfully. 'Everything is racing so very fast, like a train that can't stop, gaining speed at every turn and I keep having flashbacks to childhood and then to another time and then to another, I have no control over them and they seem so real.'

As I sobbed into the phone, I knew that this person could not take away the pain, he could not mend me; he was just a voice on a phone.

'My mind seems to want to take me to a place I haven't thought about for so very long and I want it to stop,' I added. 'I don't want to remember these things, I felt so utterly helpless then. I was happily typing chapters and the keyboard took me back, further and further,' I explained to him.

'Like painful times, Kathryn?' he said

'Well of course, dick head. I'm not talking about skipping through meadows in sunny frocks shit here, Barry!'

It was the first time I had been abusive with Barry; the phone went silent.

'No, I understand, of course you're not, I am sorry,' he apologised. I knew me and Barry were going to get along just great.

★

Case Note 2

Messy Case, client having suicidal thoughts, has had them before when she was eighteen years old. She is recalling early childhood memories of trauma. She is currently off work with stress. Client has tried to make appointment to see her GP but there are no appointments today, she will try again tomorrow.

★

Barry had a special way about him, an unassuming, humble manner. I liked this. It was like floating on a soft, gentle pillow filled with fluffy goose feathers when all around me life felt sharp, jagged and prickly. I had transported myself back into an emotional place, a situation where I had no control, a place that was about to open up feelings of intense anxiety and fear.

Email sent to work, BBC and, well, everyone really:

I looked at myself in the mirror and did not recognise myself. Even two weeks ago I had thought I looked pretty. I may have always been and not known it. Today and for the last month has been possibly one of the worst times of my life, apart from the time that I was misdiagnosed by my GP as suffering from depression when I actually had pneumonia.

I have been asking for help now for the last five weeks and still no one comes to me. This last week has been particularly difficult where I have started to self-medicate, self-refer, self-analyse and self-diagnose. Today was the worst, Barry White contacted me and we spoke, I felt better after that. I also spoke with my manager which was good too as she reassured me that I wasn't in trouble with anyone. I asked her to get me an emergency community psychiatric nurse, but then things got really wobbly so I spoke with Barry again and then contacted my manager, stating that I was going to take my life and my daughter's life. She agreed that I needed to be in hospital. Some friends came to my house to support me and then left. My other friend came to mend my boiler. Barry called back and I asked him to help me as I was really ill and he did. My brother came to get my daughter as I did not want her to go into care and that was difficult for her to understand what was happening which distressed me further. I was then contacted by the out of hours social worker who told me to go to hospital, which I did. I waited for half an hour to see the receptionist; I waited a further half an hour to see the triage nurse. I saw the triage nurse who was very rude and aggressive for which I shall be making a formal complaint about when I am well again. I had a fag and contacted family support out of hours as I was scared for my life.

My brother came to A & E and waited with me for a further three hours and still no one came. I am now back at home and in a real muddle, I will not go into hospital now as I do not trust this health service at all and do not wish to speak with anyone else other than Barry. I am staying in my room now, forever.

'Five minutes left, Kathryn, then I will be going off shift,' he announced.

I was getting used to Barry. It had been three weeks since I first spoke to him and I knew he understood me. We had an unwritten set of rules where he would let me know in advance that it was coming to the end of my time on the phone with him. We had an unspoken respect for each other, too, and no matter how angry or upset I got with him, he hung in there with me. He knew he was being used as an aid to walk me through this journey and he didn't mind.

'No, Barry, please don't go, please,' I begged.

'You know I have to go now, Kathryn. Do you remember I told you when we first spoke that I am diabetic and have to eat often?' he replied.

That always softened me, I didn't like to think anyone would be hurt because of my actions and this was also the rule I definitely had to stick to. I said my goodbyes and terminated the call.

I switched the computer on and, as I did, a whirling sound came from the back of it. It wouldn't load up; it was broken.

SIX

Case Notes
April 30th 2004

Case Notes 4

Client phoned again, she has not been able to get an appointment with her GP again, says that the receptionists are very rude and she can't cope with making calls to them. Client states that she was in a supermarket today and heard on the radio that there was a whistle blower in Sheffield. She believes that this is her and feels that the government may not like what she is saying about the state of things in her community.

★

Over the course of a few days, much to the annoyance of everyone around me, I had started to take notes on absolutely everything. Anything that happened, anything that was said, unsaid, thoughts, feelings, memories, absolutely everything recorded and then filed away. If there was something, significant or insignificant, it needed recording.

Everywhere I went, pen and paper went too. Around the house, to the shop, to neighbours, friends, to hang the washing out, everywhere I went I would scribble sentences down on paper. Conversations on the phone were noted and filed in the Phone Call section of what had become my home-made external hard drive: the bedside table.

I made notes on my daily ablutions, every time I washed, dressed, dried and deodorised. Each time I visited the bathroom, it was to be noted down in careful margins laid out in parallel columns with each day of the week carefully written on the top of each page on a small blue notepad. I registered everything I ate, noting carefully whether it was a protein or a carbohydrate, and including its calorific value. Everything had designations and everything was in order. Just as I had kept meticulous records on clients at work, I was now keeping case notes on myself. And just as Barry was keeping case notes on me, I was also keeping case notes on him.

Understandably, it had really started to piss people off. Those who didn't understand stopped wanting to be in my company, and it gave those who didn't want to be in my company a good excuse not to be. People became nervous and anxious of what I would do with all this information. Amused by the realisation that they thought their words and sentences were so intelligent that I was stealing something of great importance I carried on, filing each full page under 'another load of shite'.

Friends asked to view the illegible musings. Having nothing to hide, I willingly allowed them to look at my works. To their amazement, the muddled sentences of part conversations made no sense to anyone, not even me. Frantic at the thought that I may lose even one word that fell from the lips of others and myself, I kept on writing. I documented everything, not knowing why remembering was so important but knowing that my mind had become full. It was jam-packed from corner to corner with things to try and retain, overburdened by complicated work issues that I could no longer affect; piled high with utter nonsense that was no use to anyone, least of all me.

'Need to visit the Medlows family'; 'got to write the Case Conference report on this child that child, this family that family'; 'ring this person and that person'; 'do this do that'.

Despite all these thoughts, there was no action for I had been reduced to this mumbling, jumbling mad woman, logging and recording things that mattered to no one. My brain had reached maximum capacity, overloaded and crowded.

Careful in their speech to avoid disclosures of any kind, friends and acquaintances became distant and aloof. This was not a good time to be losing friends. As more people distanced themselves, isolation became the norm and I spent more and more time alone. My hypergraphia and I began a new relationship, like neighbours living side-by-side for years without speaking, suddenly forced to connect when disaster occurs.

My deeply suppressed feelings were surfacing, growing and developing. I felt as if I was being tossed about on a ship in stormy waters as my emotions theatrically oscillated between funny, playful and light-hearted to dark, inappropriate and desperate. I was both ecstatic and angry at the same time and felt both love and hate towards the people around me. Laughing and crying simultaneously, I sank onto my bed, onto my ink-stained, white cotton sheets. I was alone; alone in my room, alone with my thoughts and alone with my phone.

Barry and I had been talking for some time now and I was starting to feel as if life had less meaning without him, like our connection was part of a divine plan. I felt sure that Barry had been put in my path for a reason and that reason was yet to unfold. We were like 'twin flames', destined to seek each other out, no matter how far away they are from each other, no matter our personal situations. We would have always found each other. It was our destiny, our path in life and fate had brought us together and nothing, nothing could tear us apart.

We, or rather I, talked endlessly on the phone.

Spontaneous, mischievous humour was injected into our conversations as I told him 'not to go changing Barry, don't change the colour of your hair, you always were a fashion freak', and he couldn't help but laugh out loud.

Barry was reserved and much calmer than me. I wondered whether he was also getting carried along on the sea of love like I was; surely he felt it, too. The humour carefully balancing the sadness, on the seesaw of madness, covering up the distress but yet revealing the connection I still had with life itself. He tried so hard to hide his amusement with me, but couldn't.

As much as he would try and conceal his fits of laughter by putting his hand over his mouth, the more it would make me want to make him laugh and the more he laughed, the more mischievous I became. I sensed he liked the control I had over him, telephone comedy dominatrix. Barry was in the dungeon of eternal hell. He sat at a desk in a row with twenty to thirty other people around him, wearing a headset in a call centre, forced to listen to hours and hours of abuse and absurdity from people who are experiencing crisis. And then there was me. He was submissive towards me in every sense of the word and I knew it.

'Barry, you will never, ever be as funny as me, no matter how hard you try, so don't even fucking try'. Or, 'Barry, no matter how many failed marriages you have, financial problems you are experiencing, redundancy, homelessness or bereavement, I am not interested, this is about me and only me, you are there solely to make me happy so get used to it.'

He understood perfectly!

His intentions were good and he did strive to make me better from whatever I was suffering from but I didn't know whether this was indeed something that could be cured in the conventional sense. He had attempted to open up a few discussions with me about what he thought might be the problem. First of all he batted around the idea of me having

Asperger's Syndrome due to my apparent rigid thinking and my perceived problems with socialising. He mentioned the idea of me having some sort of Post-Traumatic Stress thing going on, none of which I liked the sound of.

I had my own ideas of what I thought was happening to me. This 'thing' felt like a breakthrough, not a breakdown. Something major was happening and it felt scary and exciting. I had a glow within me, a brilliant white glow that emanated from deep within my soul and it was trying to connect to something; I thought that something was Barry.

I knew that I had had enough of living in this restricted, highly charged and negative state governed by people who thought they held all the power both in my personal and professional life. I knew I hated being constantly burdened by other people's traumas and other people's issues. I needed to save myself from suffocating, from drowning in the madness of life as a social worker; a one-dimensional existence filled with sadness and grief, but knew I wasn't able to consciously throw off the shackles as there was too much at stake: the house, the job, the mortgage, the dreaded student debts.

None of that mattered though as there was a higher force at work. My conscious thinking had been blocked and the unconscious mind had taken over. It was now in charge and its force was mighty. Not fully understanding what was happening, I named it as an illness which seemed a bit odd given that it didn't feel like a cold, it didn't feel like a tummy bug or anything else that I associated with illness but I knew that I was suffering something and felt the suffering was sometimes too great to perhaps fully sit back and enjoy the ride. I tried to read the signs that were being placed before me each day but doubt kept jumping in. I couldn't visualise how any psychotherapist was going to be able to fix me up. Like a cart on a rollercoaster setting off on a 600ft descent, fast and scary with no way of dismounting the moving vehicle. I knew

I would never return to that place again; this was the start of something new. Society was not going to like this but the thick and dense chaos that was pouring out all over the place was happening, and I had no way of curbing or stopping it. I didn't want to return to my old life, I couldn't cope with it, but at the same time I hadn't prepared for the new one either.

Barry and I talked at length about the fact that what I was putting in my mouth might not be helping with the 'breakthrough'. Barry had carefully and graciously suggested a new diet regime and suggested I take the Jammy Dodgers, brandy and cigarettes off the menu.

'Why don't you go shopping for some healthy food, Kathryn?' he asked.

I hadn't shopped for serious things like food for quite a while. Faye had been dining out on chips and sausages for the last four months. I couldn't remember the last time I peeled a carrot or cut up some broccoli, I felt scared of leaving my bedroom never mind leaving my home, scared something might fall off me – like my head – or something might fall out of me – like abuse. I needed Barry to do a 'walk through' shop with me, a shop where he would remain on the phone whilst I piled food into my trolley. Barry was more than a telephone counsellor; today he had doubled up as my personal shopper.

First thing in the morning I prepared to leave the house to go shopping.

'If you try and take the brandy out of the equation and put the filters in, Kathryn, then you might start to feel a bit better,' Barry said gently, whilst trying hard not to sound as if he was putting his own value judgements upon me. I knew I had been smoking too much. In fact, any cigarettes were too much as I knew they could kill me, I had a lung condition that was not going to get any better. Barry was good at allowing me to make choices, gently guiding me to my own conclusions and decisions.

I'd been in my bedroom for what seemed like an eternity. I didn't know what would be waiting for me: cheers and applause from the masses or snubbing, people turning their backs on me. It was only two days ago when I had been shouting ridiculous statements from the bedroom window at innocent passers-by: 'Leave the Beckhams alone!' for reasons that weren't even clear to myself.

I made my way down the stairs and into the car and checked that everything was still in the right place, that someone hadn't nicked the steering wheel, the chassis hadn't fallen through the bottom of the car, and that the tyres hadn't gone flat whilst I had been somewhat occupied with other things.

Off I drove to Asda. It was still early and I wanted to avoid the queues. I despised the queuing, and loathed the trolley clingers, the four kids and a husband unenthusiastically hanging on to all sides of the trolley being rammed round the supermarket at an infuriatingly slow pace whilst the only engaged party gleefully filled up the wheeled unit to the max with the latest cut-price bargains. I never really knew where my head was going to be at or whether I could cope and keep my cool enough not to shout obscenities or smash into their piled-up families on purpose to show that shopping was not a family outing but a necessary act in order to survive. Late-night shopping was a much easier and much less stressful practice.

As I entered the shop, I dialled Barry's number for the fourth time that day and it was only 9am. I always hated having to go through the main reception to get to him, it gave the impression that it was a service, impersonal and measured, because it didn't feel like that for me. I didn't want to be just an 'outcome' or a 'service user'; I wanted to be Barry's 'special' friend. I deserved to be Barry's special friend. He was, after all, my soul mate or twin flame. He was becoming an extended version of myself and almost certainly a permanent fixture in my life.

'Barry is that you? I am here, in Asda. Now, where shall I start?' Things that had once been routine had now become alien, foreign. I didn't like it as it was taking up too much of my writing and thinking time.

The trolley's wheels weren't working properly and, as I pushed one way, it veered the other. Infuriated by the shopping equipment I continued to ram the trolley onwards and upwards. Barry was doing his level best to keep me from throwing melons at innocent passers-by.

'Well, why don't you think about fruit and vegetables that you like,' Barry said as I pushed harder and harder to move the damn trolley in the direction I needed it to go. Into my trolley went asparagus, beetroot, mineral water and all kinds of healthy detox foods. Barry stayed on the phone, guiding me down the aisles, and then he had to go. I guess, for him, it was never going to be easy getting away with reading through an entire shopping list whilst at work, in case they thought he was branching out into food ordering for the insane and helpless. I knew one thing, and that was that I didn't give two flying fucks what 'they' thought about us. I was in my own little world with Barry – Barry land – and despite the fact that he was employed by an agency as a telephone counsellor; I knew he was really my personal counsellor who happened to have the unfortunate role of also being an employee of a multinational agency.

Panic set in when I reached the checkout. The queue was long, and waiting patiently was not something I felt I could achieve. I searched for the least busy till.

Please don't strike up a conversation with me; please do not look at me; please do not speak to me! I thought to myself as I got nearer and nearer to the check out. I placed my super foods on to the conveyor belt and prayed to God that the checkout guy wouldn't speak to me. He was a young lad with a spotty face and ginger hair. I thought about the mundane role he had in society and wondered whether a less stressful job like scanning food rather than being a Child Protection Social Worker would have suited me better. I knew that once I had started talking to him, I wouldn't be able to stop, and Barry would almost certainly be central to the conversation.

Trying my best not to have eye contact, I fumbled in my trolley and placed all the items on the conveyer belt. I wondered if he could tell that I wasn't very normal. I looked down at my jumper to check if there was a label saying 'NUTTER' stuck on it. My heart raced and beads of sweat posed upon my forehead.

Don't panic! Don't panic! I said to myself, my legs beginning to wobble. I placed the items into the bag, tossed a wad of cash at him and shot off as fast as the wonky trolley would allow. Feeling proud I had achieved something that did not involve writing to Barry about Barry, thinking about Barry, making a nuisance of myself to the Prime Minister or drinking.

I thought about what I should do for the rest of the day. I had been off work for some time but had no idea how long. I knew one thing: I didn't want to return. I was on a mission, and I was too busy for real work. Far too busy.

Having made the trip out of the house, there was little point in not making full use of my new freedom. I had survived the shop and now I was desperate to go swimming. I longed to soak my aching body that had been sitting in one position at the computer for weeks. Stiff and tense from anxiety, my neck was stinging and burning and my back felt permanently bent. My swimming gear had been in the car for some months along with a towel and goggles. I'd paid for a seven-year membership at the City Leisure Centre, because fanatical exercise had been a way of keeping the demons at bay. With my healthy shopping sitting in the car next to me I was determined I was going to get back up on life, to beat this thing, to be normal again.

I set off to the city swimming pool. I wanted to ring Barry to tell him that I had made yet another ground-breaking decision that morning, I was going swimming. I knew he would be thrilled, but I felt that I also had to begin to cut the umbilical cord between us just to give him time to shoot himself with his insulin, eat something and catch up with his case notes about me.

I liked the City Leisure Centre because I had always had an issue with the way I looked. I would have felt uncomfortable training next to a group of 'top models', but it was actually a place where I could go and feel alright about myself. Everyone was all different shapes and sizes, and they were serious about training rather than just posing or on the pull. I'd been a good swimmer since being a child, swimming before I could walk. However, each time I wanted to swim, the pool was always shut to the public. It infuriated me! Being one of the largest pools in the country, more often than not the city pool would be closed to the public for a combination of swimming lessons, professional training or championships events, and this had not been explained as part of the deal when I took my membership out.

I walked through the door, anxious that everyone would be staring at me. Flustered and nervous I made my way to the reception area, waiting patiently behind four people queuing in front of me. In the foyer, people in bright yellow tracksuits had gathered in one corner and, in the other, young people wearing blue tracksuits with red stripes on their arms and legs huddled together near the vending machines.

'Lane swimming please,' I said to the girl behind the desk, looking away as I handed her my membership card.

It seemed unusually full for so early in the morning.

She looked up and casually announced, 'Sorry lane swimming is not on today or tomorrow.'

'What do you mean there is no lane swimming?' I said, conscious that I sounded like I was rattling off drugs. 'Is the other pool open?' I asked in an exasperated voice.

She clearly didn't have a clue about the amount of effort and energy it had taken me to get to this place, this position where I was ready to change, ready to heal. This was what I needed, to swim, to feel the water lapping on my face, to soothe my body in the vast expanse of H2O. I was committed to getting better and I was doing it without Barry.

'Sorry the leisure pool isn't open today either, there is a problem with the chlorine,' she added, unconcerned that I was experiencing the singularly biggest event of my entire life. My illumination. My 'breakthrough'!

I stood there, momentarily wondering if I had heard her correctly.

'Are you saying that I cannot swim here today?'

I knew the answer to the question but asked it anyway, just to communicate to her how selfish it was of them not to allow me to swim. I stood in shock, like a rabbit caught in the headlights, like someone had just told me my house had burned down with all my worldly possessions gone, emotions completely disproportionate to the event.

The demon that was not far from the surface, the destructive antagonist sitting, waiting to rise within was coming and I could not stop it.

'Fuck you, bitch!' I blurted out loudly. 'Fuck you, bitch!' I repeated just in case she hadn't heard me the first time around.

It wouldn't stop. All hell was let loose and out of my mouth came, 'But I want to fucking swim!'

My volume button on the increase, and as I continued to verbally attack, I moved further and further into the centre of the foyer, a parting began to appear where people moved out of the way in fear.

'No, let me rephrase that, I demand to swim!' I shouted at

the top of my voice. The vulgarities flew out like a vile, raging bull with no enclosure.

'Open the fucking swimming baths, I want to swim!'

It almost had a melodic sound to it. 'You are my swimming baths that I pay for, and I want a service, so open the fucking swimming baths for me now!'

The Ukranian swimmers dressed from top to two in the insidious yellow, silky, shiny banana tracksuits began to panic as if I was going to pull a gun out and start shooting them all. Instead, I lay down on the floor, making sure my little flowery dress wasn't round my waist exposing my knickers, and pretended to swim whilst shouting, 'Open the fucking baths you turds!' to the tempo of Wig Wam Bam. Sweet.

The manager came to the scene and tried calmly to persuade me to go with him into the back room to discuss the problem and, quite rightly, I refused. The police weren't far behind, as if they had nothing better to do than forcibly remove mental cases from swimming pools. They came mob handed within minutes and I was promptly escorted from the premises and into a cop car. They were very nice policemen after I explained that I had been a little under the weather and promised with all my heart that I would try my hardest to behave in future.

They agreed that it is was in no one's interest to charge me, in fact they quite liked me and agreed it was slightly unfair that I had a fully paid-up membership and wasn't able to use the facilities. I told them my stories of Barry and how much I loved him. They smiled and allowed me to leave the station, caution-less.

I returned home, laughing at the thought of being arrested and how much fun the whole incident had been. I'd never been arrested before and it hadn't been such an unpleasant experience. I'd felt safe in the police cell for two hours. I'd felt calmer, as if someone had taken some control of the situation and I felt safer in my own skin. I hadn't wanted to leave, to return home to the place where I had become a bad parent, the place where no one wanted to be, not even the cat, who had taken up residency at a neighbour's house.

The reality of the situation had unnerved me a little though. I knew that I could laugh out loud in inappropriate situations but I had never known quite how angry I could be, how uninhibited my angry outbursts could be and that scared me, for a while at least. I placed the shopping in the kitchen and returned to my room. I pushed the 'on' button on the computer, opened the disk drive and calmly placed Billy Ocean, The Very Best Of, sat back, lit a cigarette and began to write another chapter to the sounds of 'Red Light Spells Danger'.

The book that was meant to be a present for Mum for her seventieth birthday had now become a book about Barry and me. I was falling in love and I had to find a way to communicate this feeling to him. I needed a secret way, a way in which only he and I would know my true feelings. I needed a chapter with a hidden message.

Book for Barry
Chapter Thirty-Five

Happy Hour Again

Drew had quickly come to the conclusion that she quite liked being mentally ill. It was cathartic, and it gave her the absolute right to behave in whatever manner she chose. She had realised that being on the other side was equally as hard as being in the centre, as there were no services in the country that could adequately support her. Fortunately, Drew had many friends in her farm; in fact she had a zoo. And in this time of great need, Drew turned to the pigs and sheep for help.

They talked to the cows and chickens and told them that Drew was hurting and afraid, and they in turn took her plea to the wise owls and giraffes.

There was one animal in the farm that Drew particularly liked. She had seen him across the field on a number of occasions but there was a wire separating them. She would stand at the corner of the field and talk to him at dusk when her baby was sleeping. His name was Larry. Larry was a bold, sturdy looking Montadale with a beautiful coat made of the finest wool. Larry was a classic example of how the qualities of the western white-faced sheep had been bred with the popular mid-western sheep, producing the classic mutton-type features.

Drew was a Columbia. E.H. Mattingly, who was a commercial lamb buyer in the early part of this century and obsessed with the idea of producing the ideal sheep.

Drew and Larry were the ideal sheep; they had both been bred with careful hands and had common characteristics. In the endless conversations they had over the wire fence, they laughed and they cried together, but they could not touch each other and that was really what Drew wanted. She wanted to be touched by Larry, but she knew that one day the farmer would take down the wire and let them loose in the same field.

Larry had helped Drew to see that other angry animals that want to eat her could be avoided, and that it was possible to be happy in the field with all the other animals who were kind and supportive of her. She did not need approval any more, she had Larry and her other animal friends.

Drew and Larry had fallen in love. Their destiny was unclear but that did not deter them, for as long as the farmer kept them side-by-side they were happy.

With a click, the email was sent to Barry and I couldn't wait for his reaction. I was sure that he would like this one, the one that would explain to him my feelings and to seal my destiny as his 'special friend'. I also knew, deep down, that I was walking on dangerous territory. He worked for an agency and I didn't like that. I couldn't get to him every time I needed him and that drove me to distraction but, for now, I had words and words would keep us connected.

*

Case notes 5

Client appears to be completely absorbed by me and has started to write chapters to me about me. Client appears to be very delusional and psychomanic. Client is laughing uncontrollably and tells me that she can't stop 'laughing and dancing'. She has created a world in which only her and I exist and has developed us both into fictional characters

*

Case notes 6

Call to client after receiving many emails from her. She is writing again, presumably after having her computer fixed.

This client has made extensive use of this service as she has experienced a mental health episode. She continues to have insights to a degree of her situation, although this ranges in terms of her ability to handle it. She presents at times as being very much in control and at other times very out of control with long episodes of swearing. She has also indicated that she has suicidal thoughts. She has now been linked with the community mental health team who are currently assessing her.

*

Finally, an appointment to see a psychiatrist arrived in the post. I had never been to see a psychiatrist before and wasn't sure what to expect. The time had come to find out whether this was just a normal part of growing up or whether I had gone stark raving bonkers. If I had gone bonkers then they would surely be the people who would know how to fix it. I had had a really rough couple of nights and my anxieties were at an all-time high.

Feelings of wanting to hurt myself had begun to surface. I visualised myself driving really fast down the motorway and letting go of the steering wheel. I'd often had these 'what if?' thoughts but had never acted on them: 'what if I just let my body fall forwards off this cliff?' or 'what if I went under water and took a gulp of water and didn't come up for air?' I did once try and act on a 'what if' by stepping out in front of the number 48 bus as it hurtled down East Bank Road, only what I hadn't planned for was the bus turning the corner just before it hit me.

I had never been good at suicide. With my entire body having been marinated in Napoleon's cheap French brandy and my brains suitably pickled, driving was not a good option. I phoned the mental health team and explained the predicament; eventually they agreed to order a taxi for me. I arrived ten minutes early and paced up and down in the waiting room, palms sweaty and heart thumping like crazy.

'Dr Khan will see you now,' the lady on reception said to me, 'it's room four, just down the corridor,' and she pointed to a long, uninviting corridor ahead of me.

Sensing I had no idea where room four was and that I was in a pickle, she got up from her chair and escorted me to a large room with an open door. Inside the room sat a young Asian doctor who half rose to his feet to shake my hand, whilst holding onto his pad and pen with the other hand. As he sat back in his chair, he gestured for me to take a seat opposite.

The orange room was large, with many chairs arranged in a circle, and a cold, impersonal high ceiling. The environment unsettled me; the scale troubled me. Like the still life picture of Stefano Busonero measuring just three millimetres by three hanging singularly in the Louvre, it was all wrong. The space between us was uncomfortable, not conducive for therapy as I needed a microscope just to see his face. My expectations of therapy had been formed mostly by American sitcoms. Patients laid down, or sitting in soft, comfortable arm chairs designed to extract all their deep dark secrets, not perched on the edge of a hard, plastic, uncomfortable, old-school dining chair waiting to be diagnosed, repaired and sent on my way.

The session commenced. Barry was relieved that this day had finally come; maybe he could get on with some proper work knowing I was in safe hands and getting the right treatment. He could breathe a sigh of relief that all his hard work – from trying to get my own GP to sit up and take notice and actually make a referral to secondary care, to the hard task of actually getting Sheffield Mental Health Team to act on that referral, whilst single-handedly keeping me from killing myself – had paid off.

The appointment was not what I expected. It was clunky and uncoordinated, not a therapy session, but rather a simple fact-finding exercise. He spoke in broken English, which made it hard for me to understand what he was saying. A quietly-spoken, gentle man, I struggled to hear what he was saying, having to ask him to repeat sentences which exacerbated an already highly irritable state. What I didn't understand was why I was telling this guy the basic information that he surely already had, such as my name. I had stupidly made the assumption that the agencies had shared information and that someone had seen fit to take notes. How wrong I was.

I also didn't understand why he wasn't able to read my mind, that using words had become exhausting. I tried the best

I could to explain what was happening to me and to describe the events of the last few months, but this was hard; not only was there a communication problem, but so much had happened that I couldn't remember, and there were parts I didn't want to talk about, like the fact that I loved Barry White.

Dr Khan repeated what I had said to him but it didn't sound anything like what I had said; it was his own version, not mine. After the draining process of basic information gathering I was left feeling disheartened. I was informed that it was only an assessment but he would like me to return in a week's time to see another psychiatrist, Dr Walker. I had misunderstood that this guy was an understudy, his role only to assess. For me, this now meant that I would have to go through the whole story again with someone else in a week's time. I didn't know if I could survive another week like this, in the community with Faye without help. I didn't know what I was capable of. They called me a taxi and I left the building upset and annoyed, very annoyed. I was starting to feel suicidal.

Later that evening, I dialled the number to speak to Barry. He was on shift. With no 'hello' or 'how are you?' I plunged in feet first with my burning disclosure.

'Barry, there is something I need to tell you.' I knew what was coming and I knew it was wrong but I couldn't help it. He also knew what was coming and I sensed that he wanted to stop me, stop me because he knew we were being recorded; stop me because he knew he couldn't reciprocate, not in that moment, not in that role. It was the wrong place and the wrong time for us and he knew it.

'I'm in love with someone Barry.'

There was a silence on the phone. I knew that silence; Barry was lost for words.

'Who is that, then?' he enquired, knowing deep down it was him I was in love with.

'You, it's you I'm in love with, let's see if you note that down in your boring, stupid little case notes Bazza. God, you are so fucking boring,' I added, before placing the phone back on the stand. I lay on my bed to cry.

★

Case notes 7

Client apologised for her behaviour over the weekend and all her swearing. She says that she has contracted Tourette's syndrome recently. Client has been in touch with the community mental health team and they are having a meeting in one weeks' time, which she feels very angry and upset about as she needs help now. She was very angry and frightened this weekend. Thoughts of childhood experiences racing through her mind and upsetting her. Feels that being mental is giving her the chance to be on her own and away from the chaos of work.

Case notes 8

Client is behaving in a very extrovert manner. She believes that she is going to be a millionaire when people start to believe that she is 'beautifully insane'. Client terminates phone conversation as she tells me that I am boring.

SEVEN

A Pill for Every Ill
May 3rd 2004

Email to Barry:

You know that I need to speak privately about my desires for you.

Response from Barry:

I keep your emails on the computer that I use. The computer itself is used by more than one person and I don't own the space so there are no guarantees of any kind. In addition if I thought that there were clinical reasons then I would make a point of sharing it with my manager.
Barry White

Email to Barry:

I worry about you Barry; you seem to be unhappy sometimes.

Case notes

Client feeling a bit better today. She is writing again. She says she no longer feels suicidal and is 'having fun in her community' again.

Book for Barry
Chapter Thirty-Six

'Everything looks better with a tan'

She rolled her soft hands down my spine and across the nape of my neck. Her gentle hands touched the top of my legs as she massaged her way up my inner thigh. She had a soft, responsive voice, the kind that you want to listen to forever. I asked her if it was possible that I moved in to her salon with my computer and she said it was fine, but she would not be able to massage me all day as her fingers would hurt after three hours.

I said that was fine as I will take the three hours massage followed by a pedicure, a manicure, a foot spa, a hand massage, a sun bed session, an eyebrow wax, some acupuncture and some Reiki. She informed me that they did not do Reiki as no one in Gleadless would understand what it is.

She pulled my pants to one side as she poured hot wax on my inner thigh. The wax trickled down my bottom. She held my thigh as I helped her to tighten the skin, placing a cloth on the hairy area, and rip, it was all over. Out came the tweezers and she started plucking away.

This happened on two occasions as I do have two legs.

★

I wasn't altogether sure why work had come to see me at home other than to try and tell me to stop sending mail to everyone. What was clear was that they were nervous of me, and were worried about what might come out of my mouth next.

They all flooded into my home, my manager, Occupational Health, a senior practitioner and the service locality manager. Sitting in my front room they looked nervous and awkward. The awkward silence was broken when my manager asked, 'How are you feeling, Kathryn?' anxiously testing the water. I liked her; she was a kind lady with a supportive persona. I felt sad that I had added to her workload. She was managing one of the busiest child protection teams in the city and if that wasn't enough she now had to deal with a member of staff who had gone off the rails.

'I don't think I'm too well,' I replied, careful not to disclose too much information. 'But I think I'm getting better,' I added quickly, just to allay any fears that they may have of my head doing a 360 degree spin on my neck or something mental like that.

My paranoia around work issues was high. Deeply concerned that I would be deemed unfit for the job forever, I tried my hardest to look and act normal. Losing my job would leave me in a more vulnerable position than the one that I had already found myself in. I couldn't conceive of the idea of not being able to work, not having the money to pay the mortgage and, more than anything else, not having a purpose and something constructive to do with my days. I worried about how I was going to pay off the student debts that had been lingering around my neck for years, and I feared having my home repossessed.

I tried to keep my cool. The pleasantries continued whilst they filled me in on how everyone on the team was and any funny gossip that wasn't really that funny but everyone did a sterling job of smiling and laughing at the appropriate time. It was all going swimmingly well but I knew that this was only surface chit chat.

It wasn't long before Mrs Occupational Health person put her two penneth in. The pre-rehearsed one liner: 'We think you are mentally ill, Kathryn.'

I looked at the others, who all looked at the OT, waiting for her to continue. They obviously knew that was what they had come to tell me but still seemed as though this had just fallen from her tongue.

The room fell silent and I tried to compose myself, mulling over what had just been said. Right before my eyes my life as I had once known it was slowly dissolving.

'I'm not mentally ill,' I quickly retorted, 'I'm a little under the weather and in need of a break that's all,' I said, trying desperately to hide the rage that was bubbling up inside of me. I wanted to lash out and hurt someone, hurt myself for getting into this mess, break something, cause damage but despite this surge of uncontrollable anger, I was a pacifist and hated violence and anger. I didn't want to be the thing that I despised the most.

Sensing my angry defences, the conversation moved swiftly onto how they had been trying hard to get help to me and support me, how they had been instrumental in forcing my doctor's hand to make the referral to the mental health team, and that it was my doctor who had 'sat on it for weeks'.

Pressing my fingers into my sternum I furiously said, 'Me, mental? You are joking aren't you, how can I be mentally unwell, I'm good at my job, I keep a home, manage my affairs, you did say mental didn't you?'

I knew things weren't right and I was behaving in a way that didn't fit in with societal norms, but I didn't think I had a mental illness. I wondered whether this had been part of their big plan, to disarm me, to make me feel so bad that I would give my job up and leave the team. Sensing my agitation, they stood up to leave. My manager gathered the cups together and went into the kitchen to place them near the sink. The sun was shining and as she put the cups in the sink she looked out of the kitchen window and spotted the nine-foot penis in my garden that I had built with the kids in the community out of papier maché.

'What's that in your garden?' she asked.

'It's a penis,' I answered, 'it's a message for Tony Blair.'

They looked at me bewildered and started to laugh, which helped to soften my mood, but in their eyes it had simply confirmed what they already knew. I was mad; stark raving mad.

Upset and angry by their visit, I went outside and kicked my penis over and sat on the grass and cried.

'I've never been mental before so why would I be mental now?' I muttered to myself, trying to make some sense out of what they had just said.

Everyone knew I was slightly eccentric, sometimes excitable, fun and mischievous, but not mentally ill. I had a squeaky clean track record of almost complete sanity.

I would never be able to work again, everyone would look at me and think to themselves, *Oh, there goes that mental person,* they would snigger behind my back and, worst of all my professional competence would be in question and I couldn't have that. I had worked hard to achieve what I had. I'd been through university as a single parent, working night shifts to pay the mortgage and, after taking Faye to school, I would rush to university for lectures. I'd jumped through hoops so high, as nothing had come easy. I was determined that I was not going to see it all stripped away because of one jumped up, know-it-all Occupational Health telling me that 'she thinks' I am mentally ill.

'I'll take her to court,' I said to myself whilst stomping back and forth up the garden. 'I'll take them all to f'ing court, all the f'ing lot of them.'

A few people had already mentioned that they thought it was a stress related illness. *If I am mental then I'm not surprised in this job, it's enough to make anyone mental,* I thought to myself. In many ways, social work was the right profession for me as I really did care about people. I wore my heart on my sleeve, felt things very deeply and I hated distress. I hated seeing children in impossible situations, sometimes removing them into foster care that was only temporary and unsuitable, on one occasion having to take two children back to the family home as no foster places were available. I hated that some families barely met the threshold for intervention despite preventative work that was needed and most of all I hated that the intervention for the families and children that met the threshold for support was either not forthcoming due to a lack of resources or was totally inappropriate for that family. I worried about cases I had been involved in and whether the right decisions had been taken. I worried about all the families I worked with day and night. There were some families I cared deeply for and wanted to do my very best to support them in staying together, sadly in some cases this was unsupported by the system.

It was a shock to the system to find out that as a society we cared so little for the children and families that were so desperately in need and it made me sick, sick to the stomach. What made me equally angry was discovering that there were some well-known charities that had big advertising campaigns nationally, coining in vast sums of public cash but doing little on the ground to effect change. The high thresholds for referrals to their services meant that most young people barely even got their names on a piece of paper onto someone's desk. There were kids in care that urgently needed talking therapies and play therapy but no one would work with them because they were deemed as 'too chaotic', but with every placement breakdown and no one to do meaningful work with the children, any hope of healing became further and further away and so did a normal life. We did the dirty work, we shoveled the shit and we did it on a shoe string budget whilst popping one anti-depressant pill after another to cope with it all and no one cared about the children or about us.

I paced the garden feeling unsafe in my own skin, restless and agitated, pacing one step after the other. I didn't want to be in the house but I didn't know where else to go. I phoned my friend Dawn: she was a mental health nurse; she would know what to do. She was a fairly new friend but I knew I liked and trusted her. There are some people that spend a lifetime listening and never hear and there are those who don't need to listen to hear and she was one of them. She invited me to visit her at home.

I was concerned that I really wasn't in a fit state to make the journey but decided upon chancing it. The drive was long and hard, it was like being on a driving game in the amusement arcade, cars leaping out at me from all angles. Anger, frustrated drivers overtaking at great speeds, beeping their horns at me as I trundled carefully down the parkway at a steady thirty.

On the drive to Wath, not far from where I had worked in Rotherham at Crinoline House, I passed an inviting antique shop. Out of the corner of my eye I spotted a nine-foot Elvis, several sheep, a Betty Boop and some cows all standing on the pavement. These were garden ornaments for the insane; these were for me!

I swerved the car and came to an abrupt stop outside the mysterious, dimly lit antique shop to have a closer look. Inside, it was full of a mixture of furniture and mad models of mad things – I was in heaven. A six-foot shark hung from the ceiling: these weren't your run of the mill, boring gnomes or Buddhas; these were spectacular objects.

At the back of the shop there stood the most exquisite thing I had ever seen. Standing majestically was a three-foot lighthouse, which I just knew I had to have. A man appeared and asked if I needed help.

'I want to buy that lighthouse for the person that I love, Barry White is his name.'

I could have easily got away with simply asking, 'How

much is your lighthouse?' but that just wasn't my style, I had to give him my life story.

A full, potted history of the last few months in three minutes.

'It's £120.00,' he said, after I had finished my long narrative. 'I'll take it!'

No negotiating and no bartering, just a quick sale. He carefully picked up the lighthouse and whilst I was busy coming up with my next idea of what I should do with the object, he began to wrap it in brown paper. There was little doubt in my mind that this was fate and that lighthouse was destined to be mine. This was my gift for Barry. I needed to find Barry and take this wondrous object to him as a token of my love and appreciation.

Spending the afternoon lying on her kitchen floor, eating a pile of fish and chips out of the paper, I left Dawn's feeling a little better. Dawn didn't mind me rambling on about Barry, more about Barry and then to finish off with, more about Barry. I could tell she was a little concerned about the situation but overall her assessment was that 'sanity is in the eye of the beholder' and, 'there but for the grace of god go I!'

She also commented that I was probably just a 'big fat drama queen' and that she agreed with Barry that I should with immediate effect, take the brandy out of the equation and put the filters in. With regards to Barry she thought that we were like 'two peas in a pod'. I liked that. That was exactly what I wanted to hear.

Email to Barry:

Are you back on shift today? I am not going to call you again but you can call me. I think I have caused you stress but I will keep sending you my work if you are interested.

In a moment of clarity I tried desperately to rein it back in and get some perspective on the situation.

Reply from Barry:

> *Yes I have been on duty although due to finish at nine.*
> *I have not been caused stress by you at all – the idea I guess is for us to support you as best we can in whichever way you feel appropriate and what makes sense this end too. I am here if you need to talk so I will leave it to you to ring when you want – and if I am not here Jane normally is during the early part of the day.*
> *Barry White*
> *BA BD CQSW CQCYW Dip Hyp PG Dip Couns PG Dip SFBTe*

Email to Barry:

> *Well now I am impressed. Are they all the letters of the alphabet?*

★

Case notes 9

> *Client appears to be much better today and seems far more rational than she was on the weekend. Client keeps writing things down as a way of dealing with the build-up of emotions. She has promised to keep the boundaries. Client has not been drinking for a few days but feels that she is more creative and less inhibited when she has had a drink. She feels that she is too rigid and likes to be more open and fun. Client states that she is completely in love with someone but will not say who it is and that her equilibrium is fine.*

★

It was only a matter of time before I began to be curious about where Barry lived. I knew he worked in Oxford but I didn't know if he lived there.

I wondered which street he lived on, and what kind of house he lived in. A two-bed semi? A three-bed detached or a cottage, even? I could picture him living in a little cottage with a thatched roof and a glowing fire in the front room. I pictured him sitting, glass of cognac in one hand, phone in the other, chatting away to me. Timing me so that he could make sure he had time to eat before answering the phone again. I knew he needed breaks. He was diabetic, you see, that bit I did know about him. In fact I knew four things about Barry: his name, his age, the fact he was a diabetic and where he worked. However, not happy with those four things, I needed five and just as I found out the fifth thing, I needed to know the sixth: the ultimate question – whether or not Barry was actually married.

I clicked onto 192.com. There was a cost attached to getting to know the fourth and the fifth thing about Barry, but cost was not an issue for I was rich. I typed his name into the box, Barry White in Oxford. Just as I thought this would solve a problem it seemed to create more. There were at least seven Barry Whites living in or near Oxford: a Barry White tribute band in the making.

Three of them didn't match based on their ages, two of them lived too far out of Oxford to be considered which left only two. My heart sank. I focused on one Barry who appeared to have a wife and three children. The other Barry also had a wife, but just one child. I tried to convince myself that she could have left him, or died even, before the last electoral roll, and that I must not allow anything to get in the way of what was fast becoming a spiritual pilgrimage. Even if he was married, she could surely sense the intensity of feeling that we had towards each other, which would lead one to imagine that she could do nothing to prevent the inevitable course that our love was taking. She must step aside and let the natural forces of love step in, if she exists at all.

I now had two possible addresses in my possession. The next day I phoned Barry, early. I had taken on board some of what he had said about being healthier and had got the shopping to make a proper meal but had failed miserably in my attempts to cook it. It lay in the same position as the day before, occupying the space between the cooker and the kettle.

★

Case notes 10

Client unhappy and distressed that no one is listening to her. She felt very anxious when manager came to see her at home and took occupational health along. Felt very upset that occupational health had told her that she believes she has a serious mental health condition.

★

Email to Barry:

You are the only person in the world who has a full transcript of what I have written, that's a big responsibility you know, Barry Baby!

★

Case Notes 11

This client has clearly formed an attachment to me and has created a world in which there is a relationship between her and me because I am spiritual and intelligent. She mixes up a normal relationship and a therapeutic relationship. She comes across as being socially isolated as well. Client likens herself to a famous actress and craftily asked if I thought she was attractive. Client feels that someone is laying their hands on her to keep her safe.

★

Email to Barry:

Dearest Barry, my masterpiece novel is really starting to take shape now. It has no real beginning and no real ending, and that's exactly how I like it. This will be the greatest literary read ever and we, as in me and you, will be rich, richer than you could ever dream. Sleeve Notes of a Suburban Psycho, that is the title and now for the grand finale, I'm gonna give this country some public lessons on screaming and shouting. Good Bye x

★

Pacing up and down, not knowing what exactly to do with myself other than drink, write, and ring up Barry, I decided it would be a good idea if I had a swimming pool of my very own. I knew that, with my newfound wealth, I would soon be able to afford a house with its very own swimming pool where we could have great parties but until then I had to make do with one that would fit in my garden. I had seen adverts for some amazing, doughnut-shaped pools from B&Q that were being advertised on the TV. I needed to have one and, like with most things in my life, there was a real sense of urgency.

I went to the shop and placed the order. They didn't have any in stock at the time and said that it would be delivered in

100

three days. I had started to feel good about things, but that would prove to be short lived as the next crisis loomed, which would plunge me into another dimension altogether.

The boiler had broken down. Now, to most people, a broken boiler is a pain in the arse, a problem that needs fixing, a total inconvenience, but to me it was more than that – this was the straw that broke the camel's back and, after the series of annoyances and disappointments that had led to this one, I underwent a final loss of patience, temper, trust and hope.

Standing in the kitchen half naked, clutching my stomach about to explode, I knew my child was not safe around me. I knew in that moment that I could not cope any longer, that I was not safe to be left alone caring for a child and needed to be taken into hospital.

I was now three months into this crazy experience, rapidly oscillating between high mood and low, between silly and suicidal and rapidly losing touch with reality and I still had no help, still no diagnosis, still no one to talk to other than Barry and still no one to really get to grips with what was happening at home. I had to get Faye out of the house but didn't trust anyone to look after her. With no one in the family apart from my mother who had ever spent any time with Faye, leaving her with them was not an option, not that they had offered. Mum was too unwell and would not have coped with Faye, who had become increasingly difficult to manage. I cursed her weak and pathetic father for abandoning us when she was three days old – to live with his mistress who later became his wife – and I cursed social services for not supporting us, a family in crisis.

Barry was running out of options. He thought it might be a good idea for me to go to hospital, believing that I would get some treatment. Phone calls back and forth took place over the next hour whilst he tried to arrange for someone from psychiatric services to meet me at the hospital. I arranged for

Faye to stay with friends for a few days, and for another friend to take a look at my boiler, who also doubled up as a taxi driver to the hospital. I felt that this was going to be a good thing; I was going to get the help that I needed to keep us both safe. The waiting room was packed and, after an hour's wait in A&E, I was offered a mini assessment by a triage nurse who had little patience for anything that didn't involve a physical symptom. I was then left in the waiting area for a further three hours.

★

Case notes 11

This client has had extensive contact with us now. She is very distressed that she presented at A & E last night for a psychiatric assessment. After a four-hour wait she had to leave the hospital because there were parents of some children that she had previously been involved with at A & E and they spat at her. Client had been sat outside the hospital on the floor in a very distressed state. She had made a phone call to the family support out of hours service for assistance but her brother had arrived to collect her at 2am. Back up counsellor was under the impression that she had asked to leave the hospital. Client is not aware of services in Sheffield that may be able to help. This could be partly due to her confusion, or an unconscious wish to push help away. This client is a social worker so she should have knowledge of services available. In any event this client appears to be asking for help but not getting it

★

Anxious and irritable, and unable to sit, lie or stand without moving about, I climbed onto the bed and tucked my legs under my chin. It was 3am and I knew it was pointless phoning the counselling phone line: Barry wouldn't be there and I had no faith in the other counsellors. I knew I needed desperately to be in hospital but how and when I was going to get there, and who would look after my daughter whilst I got better, were two questions that remained unclear. I was trapped between a rock and hard place, I wasn't well enough to stay here in bed but equally it was impossible to leave home.

David Soul and The Stylistics had been replaced by Baroque, Pan Pipes for Lovers and Vivaldi. The meditative, deeply soulful sounds made me think about death, about what it would feel like to leave this world forever. I thought about what it would feel like to be absent of the pain, at peace, to remove myself from the world into where pain no longer existed. I put on Baroque piano concerto No 6 in F Minor and thought about what I had around me, in that very moment, that could be used as an effective tool to transport me into the world I was destined for.

Frightened by these thoughts, I picked up the phone and dialled social services in a desperate attempt to find a number for the 'out of hours' mental health team. It was going to be hard speaking to someone new, as my words weren't making sense, my sentences disorganised and abstract – but I hoped and prayed that they would understand.

A woman answered the phone. It sounded as if I had woken her up from a sleep and momentarily I felt bad for contacting her.

'I'm in a mess and things have got really silly and out of hand,' I said. 'The Co-op no longer stocks prawns and I'm not safe to leave the house.'

I knew from work that you had to be a level three social worker to work on out of hours duty, which meant you had extensive experience working in all aspects of social care. I also knew it was well paid, much better than the peanuts other social workers were getting.

'I think you need to just go to sleep,' she responded in an angry tone.

I was not expecting that at all.

A moment of clarity came over me. 'How dare you speak to me like that? Do you know that I also work in the profession and it's this profession that has fucked my head up?'

I slammed the phone down and felt at an utter loss as to where I was going to go next or what I was to do. Then the phone rang: it was the woman I had just been speaking to.

'I am really sorry, I didn't realise you were a social worker!' she exclaimed.

'Well I didn't realise how hard it would be to be mentally unwell either you, you…' I wanted to give her a swear word name but resisted. I continued, 'What would the difference have been if I wasn't a social worker? I'm in mental distress and I have tonight tried to get myself admitted into hospital and failed miserably. And now I am back home, oscillating between suicidal and elation like I have never experienced before!' I bellowed down the phone.

'Are you bipolar?' she asked.

'I don't know what the fuck I am, but I am deeply pissed off that I have had to pay someone to look after my child because I know I am a danger, and not one person is in the slightest bit concerned that I might hurt myself or her.'

With that I put the phone down. I was running out of patience with people paying lip service to help and nothing ever happening; I was running out of steam trying to tell services what was happening. It was all give and no take and I had had enough.

I got out of bed, went downstairs and took a knife from the wooden holding block on the windowsill. There was no one in this city with any sense to see what was happening here. It wasn't fair on Faye and it wasn't fair on my friends. I grabbed the electric tape from the drawer and returned to my room, sat on the bed and placed the knife on my wrist. It wasn't the sharpest knife in the world and the idea of slitting my wrists had never seemed a very attractive way of killing oneself. I thought about slitting my throat but knew it would leave an awful mess if I wasn't successful, and that I would have to wear a neck band for the rest of my life. It wouldn't have suited me.

I kneeled on the floor, tape in one hand, knife in the other and began taping the base of the knife to the floor. They had shown us many things on *Blue Peter* in the 70s: I'd learned to build a Tracey Island, a Dalek out of cardboard loo rolls and a cat string holder out of an old washing up liquid bottle.

But, unlike the 'one I made earlier' *Blue Peter* masterpieces, my do-it-yourself 'kill yourself' kit was not something I had ever needed to learn how to make before. The idea of the 'sticky up knife' affair was an altogether crap invention that was doomed from the start. The idea was for me to fall on it, the knife cutting neatly through my stomach whilst I faded away calmly and quietly.

It hadn't occurred to me how hard this would be to fall on a knife that was flopping around like a sheet in the wind. If the falling part was hard, keeping the knife in place was even harder. The first attempt I fell and achieved only a massive bang on the head as I missed the knife completely and smacked straight into the side of the bed. The second attempt was even worse; forced falling is harder than it seems. It was a pathetic attempt at suicide and I gave it up and curled up in bed to try and rest for a few hours.

★

Email to Barry:

> *Do you know what I am thinking, I am convinced that you are in my head and know all the moves that I make in the day*

even though I only have about four. Are you in work today?
Please ring me. I nearly fell asleep today but you know me I
like to talk too much and if I'm asleep, I can't talk. I'm going
to send you my next chapter now.

★

Another day and another rapid mood swing. A week had
passed since I last saw the psychiatrist's understudy and that
morning the phone call that I had been waiting for had finally
come: an appointment with a proper, fully-qualified shrink. I
was certain that, this time, they had everything they needed to
treat me, to tell me what was wrong and help me get back to
being normal again. Again they sent me a taxi, and I waited
patiently in the waiting area to see her. I dressed smartly,
wearing my black dress and overcoat as I didn't want her to
think that I was a total mess. I took her some chapters of my
book for her to look at to see if she could decide what on earth
was happening to me as I didn't have a clue anymore.

I entered the room and sitting at a desk was Dr Walker.
She was a middle-aged woman who had an air of authority
about her that made me feel uneasy.

The room was much smaller this time, like a cubbyhole, a
place to hang coats and put shoes. There was no couch, only
an uncomfortable plastic chair that reminded me of the chairs
we had at school in the dining hall. When she asked, 'What
can we do for you Kathryn?' my heart sank, for she was yet
another person in the ever-increasing line of people who I had
come into contact with that had no fucking idea about what
was happening.

How the hell was I supposed to know what they could do
for me? I tried as best I could to explain things to her, just like I
had the previous person and everyone else, but was careful not
to disclose too much about my feelings for Barry. I knew Barry

loved me like I loved him and it would ruin his career if people found out. I didn't know whether she was a safe person or not.

'What have you brought?' she asked inquisitively; looking down at my lap where I clutched the chapters I had written. She showed little in the way of warmth, which made it hard for me to open up to her.

'I'm writing a book.'

I leaned forward on my chair and reluctantly handed her the wad of paper. 'It's about someone I love.' I spoke softly to cover up the deep feeling that seemed to be coming from my solar plexus.

'Who is it? Is it a boyfriend?' she asked. She took the paper from me and glanced over it briefly and disinterestedly.

'Not yet,' I replied, 'though I haven't a hope in hell's chance with this person when I am so ill like this,' I added.

'Well, let's see if we can make you better then, shall we?'

I felt a little more at ease with her with those words, like she cared about what was happening to me and was in her own way trying to connect with me on some weird level. I explained a little about work and the stresses I had felt working with such a high level of negativity and emotional upset. I wanted to talk to her about whether what I was experiencing was love. I wanted to know if these crazy emotions were a sign I had been connected to my soul mate but I daren't.

'You will never be able to return to that role, you do know that don't you?' she said abruptly.

I hadn't planned for this, to be told by someone who I had spent only a few minutes with that the career I had worked so hard to achieve and given so much of myself to was now over. I wanted to cry but didn't want to give her the satisfaction.

'I'd like to see you again in a week's time Kathryn,' she said. I could not believe that I was being left like this for another week. I wanted to say to her that this was not a safe situation but the words just would not come out of my mouth.

'I feel really unwell,' I muttered to her, trying to get her to understand the severity of the situation.

'I don't think hospital is the place for you, Kathryn, we can try and get you sorted in the community.' And with that she stood up and began moving towards the door.

What about my thoughts on this being a spiritual awakening? What about whether I have found my twin flame, what happens if it's not OK? I thought to myself as I was being ushered out. I felt panicked and sick.

'Bring someone that knows you well next time if you like, it would help to give us an idea of what's going on for you.'

I didn't have anyone that really knew everything that had been happening. All my friends were really busy with their own lives and I hated to burden them with this. I wanted Barry to come but I knew he couldn't.

EIGHT

The Pool of Madness
Sometime in May 2004

Book for Barry

'Barry, in your eyes I see ribbons of colour, I see us inside each other, I feel my conscience merge with yours. I'm falling for you,' Drew told him. 'I was afraid of letting you in. The walls started to tumble down and I couldn't see the ground,' Drew said softly. 'I'm falling like a leaf, like a star, catch me don't let me drop,' she said desperately, longing for his warm, soft hands to hold her gently.

*

Strange and wonderful things were starting to happen to my computer. Each time I reached for the mouse, the cursor would move slowly across the screen. Nervous about the fact that I may be 'wide open' and unprotected, I started shuffling documents around. I knew that my book was worth millions and knew that there would be people who would go to any lengths to get their hands on a copy.

It was only a matter of time.

Everywhere I went, there were signals: radio, TV, shop signs and notice boards all seemed to have meaning, as if they were leading me to something – but I wasn't sure what. Higher forces were at work, but I couldn't work out what they were trying to tell me. The word 'patience' appeared most frequently. 'Patience' and 'you have it all'.

I took this to mean that I needed to be patient for all good things to come to me and that I needn't worry about making things happen anymore as I had it all already, all the pieces were there they just needed fixing together. I felt some comfort in this but doubted that it was really true.

Things had got worse at home. Faye was staying out late and being self-destructive. Things were going missing from the house and it was impossible for me to keep track of the situation. I became intensely fearful of her friends and worried that they were playing upon her vulnerability, as she enjoyed being the centre of attention and having freedom.

The swimming pool had not been delivered like the man at B&Q had promised. Over the course of three days I made numerous calls to them and each time I was told something different.

'Your pool will be with you in the next few days,' one woman said.

'Your pool is on order and will take about two weeks to arrive', according to another woman.

And, 'Your pool is actually still in Japan, we have a problem with shipping,' a guy said as he tried to get me off the phone.

I was so angry by the time I had put the phone down to the last person that I decided to pay B&Q a visit. It was a new store and had only been open a few weeks and I liked it there. What I didn't like, though, was not having my pool. It had now been four weeks since I had ordered it. I couldn't chance going to the local baths again, who knows what might have happened? I needed to have water at home, water I could lay in and soothe my aching body, relax and feel the warmth of the summer sun.

I stood in a queue, clutching my receipt, becoming more and more impatient as the minutes ticked by. Eventually, I got to the front of the queue. I handed them my receipt for the pool.

'I would like to have a full and honest answer as to where my pool is, please,' I said, loudly and confidently. 'I have been waiting for weeks now, and you have told me several different versions of why I haven't got it and how long it will be.'

'Will you just bear with me?' the guy said as he started typing the code into the computer.

'It appears that this order has not been put through properly,' he said, worried that my face was starting to change colour as the beast was about to be unleashed once again. 'In fact, it looks like someone has cancelled your order.'

'Has it been ordered? Has it been cancelled or is it in fucking Japan, Honolulu, Africa or fucking China?' I shouted. 'I want my fucking pool and I want it now, and if you don't get me a fucking fifteen-foot pool I shall, I shall…' I took a deep breath as I really didn't know what I 'shall' do at all.

I looked round the shop and next to me there was a pile of brilliant white paint stacked up like a tepee, 'I shall…' I continued shouting, 'push this fucking pile of…' and that was it. Before I had chance to say the word 'paint', I had pushed the whole stack of tubs of paint onto the floor.

The manager came rushing over. I burst into tears and fell to the floor, in the white paint. Exhausted and white, very white. I was lifted by the security guards and taken behind the counter into the office and made to stand there while they phoned the police.

'It's out of character, this behaviour,' I pleaded with them, frightened that this was now the second time the police had been involved in less than four weeks.

'Please don't call the police!' I begged, 'They will lock me up and throw away the key as I am such a nut job.'

The manager was kind and put some plastic on a chair so I didn't get paint all over the office. Footprints followed me into the office and I could hear people coming over to look at the mess, gasping in the horror that they would have to clear it up.

'I have money, I'll pay for the damages, I promise,' I said in desperation. 'You lied to me, you see. I bought a pool that I saw on the television and I've been so very ill and just needed that pool, and your staff have been messing me around on the phone and you don't understand, it's so important that I have this pool immediately,' I pleaded.

I explained to the police that I had tried to get admitted into hospital but couldn't, and that they had now sorted me a psychiatrist out and I was to see a CPN once a fortnight. This time it didn't seem quite as funny, but once again I managed to charm my way out of a charge. They cautioned me and I agreed to pay for all damages and left the station with my white tail between my white legs.

I returned home wrapped in a plastic bin liner, with a bag full of clothes covered in paint. I opened the wheelie bin and slung them in before entering into the house. I ran a bath and laid out on my bedroom floor vomiting, spewing the cocktail of medication out. The antidepressants, the Piriton that my GP had said it was alright to take as it is a mild sedative, the Voltorol he had also told me to take as my face was swollen and sore. I wanted a cure for this mess, and if there was no cure for it then I wanted to go someplace safe, like a caravan with a carer near the sea; somewhere to heal and to be peaceful whilst remaining safe.

I didn't want pills. I hoped and prayed someone would come, someone who understood, someone who could cope with it all without making a fuss or making me feel bad for stressing them out and making them ill, but no one came.

I could not cry. I had no emotion, not knowing how to tell people, tired of trying to tell people, my anguish falling on deaf ears.

The next appointment to see Dr Walker had come around.

'I think you are bipolar, Kathryn,' she began. 'You have all the classic symptoms of bipolar disorder, the mood swings and behaviours.'

I didn't tell her about Barry. I didn't even tell her about the arrests. I felt stupid and ashamed. 'I'd like to try you on this drug,' she added.

She pulled out her prescription pad.

'Drug, what drug?' I said, slightly shocked that this was my treatment. I hadn't considered that they might just give me pills and send me off back into the community. I thought they might have wanted to talk to me about my feelings, about some of the things that have happened in my life to bring me to this place but she seemed disinterested in that.

'Olanzapine, it's an antipsychotic. Take one a day, it's only a low dose to start you off,' she added, without even looking up from the pad she was scribbling on.

'Come back and see me in two weeks – by then you will feel much better.'

She handed me the script, and I looked at the bit of green paper in my hand, shocked that in the last ten minutes I had been told I had a severe mental health condition named bipolar disorder, and that I was handed a script and sent away.

That was it. No explanation of what bipolar disorder was or how it would affect me, what to look out for, what to do or not do, nothing. Nothing but a green piece of paper. I had my own idea of what would make me better but no one seemed interested in talking to me about the underlying causes for this distress, no one but Barry.

I popped the paper into my pocket and left the room.

Two weeks later, I was offered an appointment with a

different psychiatrist, my own psychiatrist. Unlike before, when I had been shoved from pillar to post, not understanding a process where I had been assessed by so many different people, I now had contact with one person, Dr Maharajah, a Hindu doctor from central northern India. Dr Maharajah was a nice man but, once again, there was a serious language barrier, which only served to add to my frustration, due to my heightened state of anxiety. Repeating sentences over and over had become a familiar part of the process. It was all too much like hard work for me. Too much 'giving of myself' and no getting back, I seemed to be getting nowhere, gaining nothing other than weeks and weeks of visiting people, giving them information, only to be sent away no better.

I talked to Dr Maharajah about what had been happening and explained that I wasn't altogether happy with the diagnosis that Dr Walker had given me. He explained that my behaviour would suggest that I was bipolar.

I hadn't actually told anyone about Barry, about my feelings towards him, so it was based purely on other behaviours. I sat in his office and sobbed. I worried that I was flooding the place. Head in hands I told him how desperately unhappy I was.

'But why you so sad, my dear? You have lovely home, you have lovely child, you have good job, why you so sad?' I could have got that response from the checkout lady in the Co-op.

I felt a fraud. Maybe he was right! I did have all these things in my life and here I was, unhappy. Why did I have this overpowering and unbearable feeling of hopelessness? Why was I so desperately sad? I tried to explain that each day was becoming more and more of a struggle, each day the thought of just existing pained me. The world was not a place I understood anymore. Friends seemed repulsed by me, a burden that they could not take on in their own busy lives: while I was breaking down they were all trying hard to hold on.

I was assigned a community psychiatric nurse whom I saw on a weekly or fortnightly basis for about four weeks. I tried hard to keep my appointments, which wasn't hard as nothing else filled the pages of my diary. I welcomed human contact, though even getting dressed was an effort. I would sit for over an hour, head bowed down, trying to motivate myself to lift my arms up over my head.

I never missed an appointment with him as it was the only place that I felt I could go without burdening other people. However, a trip out was all it was, for nothing meaningful could be gained from any of these sessions. The only topic of conversation on the table was to do with pills. Blue pills, pink pills, white pills, I was sick of fucking pills. I wanted to talk to someone who really understood what I was experiencing, someone to tell me it was going to be alright and that normal life would eventually resume. I needed to talk to someone about what I had experienced as a child, what I had experienced as a mother but most of all I wanted to talk to someone about what I had experienced as a social worker. I needed reassurance that these experiences, this behaviour, this anger and this sadness were normal. I needed someone who I trusted enough that I would be able to open up about Barry without feeling judged or condemned in any way. And, most of all, I needed someone to properly explain the complexities of bipolar disorder to me.

Week after week I asked the same question, 'When am I going to get to speak with a therapist, like a counsellor?'

Having never been in mental health services before, the only thing I really knew about psychiatrists was that they occasionally were called upon to do reports on parents for us in court and that they could get you sectioned. I was surprised to discover that there was no comfy chair to lie back in or anyone to look beneath the surface at what might be going on. It had been months now since I was last at work, and time was running out. I'd been put on half pay and was worried that that would soon run out too. I couldn't live on that and needed to be well to return to work as soon as possible. I had no time to wait and it seemed as if they had all the time in the world to waste. Everything seemed so slow, there was no urgency for them.

With no therapeutic bed to lay on and no real understanding or compassion about my experiences, the likelihood of me being be pieced back together anytime soon was very slim.

NINE

Gone Barry Gone, Love is Gone...

Book for Barry

'He was her friend, the one she desires
But now all it is, our friendship is on fire
They would talk every single day
Now there's no words, nothing left to say
She loved him so much, that he knew. They were so
close, their friendship grew.
All she wanted was his love and affection, that couldn't
happen, he couldn't pay her the attention.
How could she love someone who just wasn't real? Did
he realise how she would feel?
Did he want her? Her love for him will never tire, but
this is the end, their friendship set on fire.

★

It had been three weeks, two days and eight hours since they
took my love away. I knew exactly what the catalyst behind
this heinous attack on me was about. I could hardly blame
anyone: I knew why I had sent it; we all knew that. Sexual
enticement, that's what it was. Bursting, peaking, glowing

man trap. Lighting the room like a thousand watt bulb. Luring him into the den of iniquity. I wanted him and I wanted him now.

That was the state of mind I was in, the one that would lead to me doing what I did, and to 'them' putting an end to our relationship.

The worst thing of all was having his email address. I wondered whether him giving it to me was his way of wanting more of me, wanting to know me better. It was obvious I would abuse it, but this consequence-free existence didn't provide buffer zones, or give me anyone to explain cause and effect to me.

Did he think I was lying when I said I had written ninety-two chapters? Did he want to read them to feel the love, to feel wanted? Did he know that our time was running out, that someone would pull the plug on our little private love affair? Or did he want to see the grand finale? To be the casual observer in the grand exit, the mess? After all, up until this point nothing had been visual or tangible. Whatever he was thinking, it led to me writing more and drawing this story to its final conclusion, its fate had been written. I was in the last-chance saloon.

Email to Barry:

I agree that you should have shown your manager the picture, I would have acted in the same way if I still had a job, but that seems highly unlikely now given my behaviour. I now presume that my post is closed and my career has come to an abrupt end.

When I make some big money Barry we can be with each other in whatever way we choose surely?

I didn't understand all those letters after your name that you sent, but you sound like a clever man and I like that in a person, you may be in love with someone but I don't know that for sure but I know that you have been there for me and that's a big thing baby!

I would like you to be with me forever but I also know that that is not possible at the present time because you are the therapist and I am the patient. Everything has got a bit strange recently. I want you to move closer to me. I keep dreaming that you make all the dragons go away. I'm sorry for being angry and abusive and swearing, I can't help myself, it has to come out somewhere. Answer me please, now Barry, NOW I said. Are you sure that I do not cause you any stress Barry?

★

Case notes

Client angry that I had shown picture of her to my manager. I explained that it was part of a boundary thing, which she finds useful and which makes her feel safe to talk. Client feels that she needs to approach a private therapist as help is not forthcoming from the mental health team. She is worried as she doesn't know how much money she has got in the bank. She thinks she may be a millionaire but daren't look. I advised her to check her bank statements immediately.

★

Email to Barry:

It's getting so fucking lonely in this bed again. I don't know if I should or could lick my wounds. There is a naked person in my head telling me that I'm not alone and that, after midnight, morning will come and I will be safe. Everything in this world is free. I'm running, running so fast, catch up with me. Why can't you see that I'm falling. I'm falling into the sky and the stars, turn off the light and see into my dreams and my nightmares. Share that with your fucking manager Barry!

★

Book for Barry
Chapter Thirty-Eight

'Up Close and Personal'

'By the magic of Venus, with the passion of Eros, I awaken the flame of desire.'

Deep within his voice, she sensed a glow of light, so powerful it shone through his words, each and everyone of them, she lingered on the endings of each sentence, longing for him to say it again, 'Breathe for me darling, breathe.' Now and again she could detect nervousness, sadness and anxiety in his voice, but he was able to hide his emotions from her.

Drew knew that she had found her soul mate. She knew that he was the one. But she also knew that she had a vulgar, offensive side that kept getting in the way. 'Up your bum' this; 'up your bum' that. 'Come up to Sheffield and shove your big fat cock in my gob' – where was it going to end? She just couldn't shut up. She was rude and foul-mouthed and she was ruining any chance of getting near to Larry. I just do not know how Larry puts up with this crap, Drew thought.

He was so anxious when he could not come to her, he wanted to hold her and make it a safe place for her, but he couldn't because he was so frightened of his feelings for her. He needed to make love to her, he needed to wrap her up in his warm coat and take her home with him in his pocket.

'Larry, I am a woman and I have needs. I may be a nutter, but I'm still a woman. I can't spell, sekrets but you can. Anything you want doing baby I will do it. When it comes down to some good old-fashioned love, that's what I have got.

'I can read your thoughts. I ain't bragging cos I'm the one, just ask me, Ill be there.

'I cant go on kissing toads, Larry. I see neon lights when you walk by. I think about the fireworks that go off when you smile. Once in a while, two people meet, and suddenly there are thunder and showers everywhere. Who can explain the thunder and rain when I'm with you?

'A few stormy moments is that all we shared, Larry? If you have your family do they really need you there. I've tried really bloody hard to resist being last on your list, Larry, but I am afraid that no other man will do. So here's the deal pal, looks like I'm saving my love for you.

'It's not easy, Larry, being in this field on my own. The pigs tell me to find another sheep, but I'd rather save my love for you,' said Drew. 'I thought we were gonna run away together Larry, you said be patient and wait a little longer but that's just an old fantasy and my patience is running very fucking thin.'

'Oh don't be such a fashion freak Larry, and for god sake don't go changing the colour of your hair. You know I have no interest in clever conversations with you, and I seriously do not want to work too hard. I just want someone I can talk to.

'I want to pull the stairs down from the sky, I want to live again and never die. I want to change the world only for you. I want to hold you close under the rain, every time you phone me I become a hero. I won't tell anyone. No one has to know, if you want to be discreet.

'Am I being slightly attention seeking, Larry? Everyone is trying to tell me what is right for me, but it's plain to see what I need. YOU!

'This world is wearing thin, stay with me Larry, move in with me, move in next door, move in anywhere you like as long as you are near. I'll tell you again and again I'm in LOVE with you Larry.'

I thought I had made that perfectly clear. I could see this was not the most sensible thing I had ever done but he had left me with no choice, Barry was just not getting the message. I took a deep breath and pressed the big shiny red 'send' button, my favourite button of all. The one I was so familiar with. With a click it was sent but there was more to come. The party was just getting started.

Book for Barry
Chapter Thirty-Nine

'The Grande Finale'

As she slipped her fingers inside herself, she pulled her hand away. There was no feeling. It felt damp and soft so she put her fingers back in and began rubbing gently. Her thoughts were muddled and confused. First it was the phone bill and then the car tax. *Stop!* she thought, *Relax, lock the door and shut the curtains. This is quiet time. This is your time.*

Alone in the blue room; the aqua room with a chamois ceiling and chocolate skirting boards; the Egyptian room. Unopened letters strewn around the room, empty bottles of pop and tubes of Pringles, files and books piled high.

There was a strong knot in her tummy; it would not

go away. It was a mixture of fear, anxiety and anger. *Stop! Relax, let it all go, drift away. Think about what makes you happy. He makes me happy, larry makes me happy.*

The rubbing started to feel nicer, more relaxed, more gentle, uncontrollably gentle and soft. The moisture ran down her legs as her body moved to a gentle rhythm.

In her thoughts he was there, softly caressing her tulip lips, then her tummy. Twisting and turning, biting, and licking her inside and out. Tasting her softness, tasting her kissing lips.

As she gently slid himself inside her, 'I am here for you my love, I will always love you, you are so beautiful, you are my angel, my only angel and I will never leave you,' he whispered in her ear. Their bodies moved in synchronicity, their sweat merged, their smell was beautiful.

And then she had the biggest orgasm of all time and the bed shook. And it was all over. She was no longer mentally ill. She was however very concerned and anxious that the nail polish had smudged on her big toe.

★

Alongside the emails, I thought it important that Barry see another picture of me, far more provocative than the last one.

With a click of the button, the email was sent. The chapters, the picture and a big fat X. I sat back and waited, and waited and waited. Then I gave in and went to the Co-op for more wine.

★

Email from Barry:

Dear Kathryn,
I would like to take this opportunity to thank you for sharing your work with me and for showing me the picture. I guess the point is that we are here to support you in the best way that we can. I have had to show my manager what you have sent in order for us to continue our support. I therefore have to inform you that a clinical decision has been made and that I have been moved to other duties.

You are welcome to continue using our service in whatever way you see fit. I hope that you have found our sessions useful and wish you all the best in the future.

Yours sincerely
Barry White Intake counsellor TNH

Silence. World. Fallen. Apart.

T E N

Loving you Dot Com

THE INTERNET HAS PROVIDED US with many gifts: the gift
of being able to connect with others all over the world, the gift
of information, education and sometimes love. For the isolated,
the internet is a saviour. However for people with mental
health issues it has mixed blessings. People connect with
others, anonymously, to live out their periods of mania or
depression without the fear of wrecking their own lives.

So there I was, still sick, still alone and still very scared.
Barry had gone, and despite his mammoth attempts to get
some appropriate help to me, I had nothing. He had been the
only person to have a full understanding of what was
happening in my home, in my head and in my thoughts on a
daily basis. Barry going had left me increasingly at risk.

People had been popping up on my computer screen for a
while and I knew they were all Barry. I don't remember
signing into anything or posting a profile up, but that meant
nothing: the short-term memory loss had been with me for a
while, my frontal lobes pickled by stress, insomnia and my
self-medicating tactics of drinking far too much booze.

I wasn't aware that I had invited anyone to my computer
but they came, and I was surer than anything in the world that
it had all been orchestrated by him. They might have taken

him from me, but his love for me was so strong that I knew he would pull out all the stops to find a secret way of communicating with me. He was clever, my Barry, oh so very clever. He had concealed his identity from the masses out to destroy him, the non-believers. This way no one would know it was him; he was incognito.

I didn't know much about Barry but I knew that he had a wild but controlled sense of humour. This was how he kept me in one place, engaged on the computer so I didn't create any more public disturbances.

Each morning, I would receive twenty, maybe thirty emails from Barry pretending to be someone else. I had been using the pseudonym 'Drew Berryfields' to talk with him on line. He was a genius, my Barry, there was nothing that he couldn't do and although he had a stressful job, he still found time to make me happy. It was all for me.

On his website an advert popped up on my screen, saying, 'Play with me'. It was obvious that this was a design of Barry's, a way of luring me in. I was in a playful mood and graciously accepted his request to play.

Barry had built this website just for me! TickleDotCom. He was so in love with me that he wanted to know as much about me as he possibly could and the obvious way to do this would be to ask me questions through quizzes. 'Are you a Fresh Momma?', 'Are you Fickle?', 'Who is your *Star Wars* twin?' All those important things you need to know when you are serious about someone.

I answered most of the 150 questionnaires and it wasn't long before Barry popped up on the screen wanting to chat. Of course he didn't want to be found out and it was also part of our 'little game' so he called himself 'Ian', not Barry. He was incognito.

'Hi, wanna chat?' he asked.

Yes I bloody well do want to chat! I thought to myself.

'Hi love, how have you been?' I replied, careful not to be gushing with enthusiasm. 'I have missed you.'

'Oh, that's nice,' he replied.

'You are Barry, aren't you?' I asked really early on just to allay any fears that this could indeed be an imposter.

'I can be anything you want me to be,' the typing appeared. *Oh he is a cheeky monkey*, I thought to myself.

'Barry, you are so funny, I'm so glad I have finally found you.'

'You have darling,' he replied, 'you definitely have.'

Sometimes he would email me in the night.

Dear Drew

Having read through your profile several times, I consider it so imperative to register my interest in you. I wish to really establish a good conversation with you either through e-mail or telephone if and only if you would be kind enough to grant my offer. I am a Nigerian national working and residing in Sweden...'

Oh Barry, you are hilarious and so very creative, I thought to myself.

Icebreakers would be sent to me by different people. Ugly-As-Sin sent:

Friend, Best Friend, Soul Mate or Lover

Who are we really looking for?
Can we go from Stranger?
To Soul Mate or Lover in a Heartbeat?
Or does that only happen in Dreams?

Hundreds of random messages kept coming. Had I been writing to Barry in my sleep I wondered? Sometimes a big circle would appear, saying I had no friends. I took offence to that because, even though I knew I had totally pissed all of my friends off by being so unbelievably draining, I knew that Barry was my friend and my old friends would reappear once I started to behave again.

The messages kept coming. Either this was all Barry or I had attracted the entire male population of the world with my photo! Of course, the photo hardly represented what I looked like now, as it had been taken two years earlier. I hadn't even looked at myself in the mirror for months; I felt brilliant, glowing and slim but I was scared to look at an image I was sure did not match my own inner perception of myself. I wasn't eating and had not been in the sunlight for months and that was not the way to look sexy at all.

I continued chatting away to Barry all night, every night. He used a range of interesting and elaborate aliases, mine remaining constant.

My heart raced on the occasions he gave me some information, information that I had long awaited to hear: he was single with grown-up children. I was pleased.

Then, an advert for a new website appeared on my screen. Its name was LovingYou.Com. The site was pink and green, symbolising gentleness and warmth. It was a site about all things *love*. The 'messing around' phase – when he was finding out as much information as he could about me – was over. He had extracted my information from the quiz website and was now presenting me with something very different; he was showing me how much he loved me.

Finally, he wanted a place to share his feelings. I pushed a CD into the PC, lay back on my bed and listened to the sweet sounds of Richard Clayderman's instrumental version of 'Endless Love'.

LovingYou.com was a site like no other. It allowed him to publish and write poetry, love songs, stories and, best of all, give me gifts. It was perfect! But it wasn't all one way – Barry had been super clever in designing me a site that allowed me to respond by publishing my own poems and love stories for him. We could buy each other gifts and, although I couldn't send them to him directly as I had no idea where he lived, he would be able to get them from his own private warehouse.

The site's shop showcased items that Barry had carefully selected for me; things that I know he would want to give to me if only he could break through the professional boundaries and come and take me to be his.

It was brilliance, pure brilliance.

The 'Love Shop' sold so many wonderful things: Mrs Berryfield's Love Chocolate, an underwear collection by Drew and many other coincidental brand names. All these things were signs telling me that it was him and this made me desire him even more. He had used his intelligence and initiative and it was paying off. This wasn't some jerk that bought a few flowers and took me to Meadowhall for a tuna sandwich, or someone who couldn't even remember when my birthday was. No, this was the real thing. Barry was spellbinding, all-powerful and omnipresent.

I started to shop. Firstly, I needed to buy Barry something to thank him for being so wonderful. I looked under the 'For Him' section and picked out a number of presents. An 'Around the World in Twelve Coffees' gift set, a 'Kenneth Coles' men's gift set, a 'Kama Sutra Massage Oil' just to get him in the mood. A 'Thinking Of You' Sienna Marble Keepsake and a toy electric boat for the swimming pool.

Then it was Faye's turn. I told her that she could have anything she wanted because we were going to be very rich. I explained that money was no object, so off she went shopping. First, she bought a 'Follow Your Heart' charm necklace, a message ring, a personalised 'Wow I Love You' bear and many other items. I purchased a few things for myself too: 'Sweet

Notions' Charmeuse Set, a 'Chocoholics Survival Kit', Lush
Karma soap, bath gel and perfume gift set and some sex
bubbles. This was serious business – spend, spend, spend – I
couldn't get enough of it. I'd seen films about men like Barry:
suave, intelligent and very rich.

Alongside setting up a website with a shop on it for me,
each day he would publish poems for me.

A special bridge was built
Displaying a welcome sign
There would be no barrier
You could reach at anytime…

It said it was by someone called 'Hope' but I knew that this
was just a word expressing the feeling that he had that one day
we would be together and happy.

It was wonderful to see Faye so excited and happy. She
believed in me and knew that if I said something was real, it
was definitely real. If things were going to happen, then I was
the person to make it happen. She believed in my character
and in my strength. I had never let her down before and I
wasn't about to begin. I was a funny, colourful and dependable
mum that always, always made sure things happened.

That night, I explored the site and started to write poems
knowing that this was, for now, the only way Barry and I
could be near each other. I knew that each day he was getting
closer to me, so close I could just about feel his virtual breath
upon my face.

I had started posting under several different names,
including Unique Unicorn and Drew Berryfields. The
unicorn symbolises a legendary animal, the symbol of grace
and purity, emblematic of love and faithfulness, yet untameable
and unwilling to be a servant to any man. Just like me. Barry
knew that about me, he would never want me to be subservient

to him. I knew that when we were eventually married, he would showcase me as his strong, fabulous beast of a woman; a true wild ass.

Show me where we are going

by Unicorn
Take my hand and lead me into your crazy wonderland
Catch me running past your window in your net of wonder....

I could finally be who I wanted to be, I could express myself fully to him without being recorded, rejected or abandoned by some jumped-up dick of a clinical manager. I was free! Free to show Barry the love I have for him, to wrap him up in my own warmth and desire. I was safe and would no longer cause trouble or upset anyone. I was with Barry.

Replies to my poems came thick and fast. Each time I published a poem on the site, several more followed, each with a different writing style and content.

For Barry Bee

When the bathroom fell through
All I could think about was you
I will give you everything for you are a STAR,
I will scrape the ice of your car,
I will travel from afar,
I will let you take off my bra.
I will bring you a gift from my heart
I will try not to fart and
I will have BW waxed into my pubic hair

By Unique Unicorn

Excited, I waited for the reply and sure enough, there it was: a poem by someone called Bryan. This had to be Barry! Bryan is so like Barry, they both began with B and had an R and a Y in there.

The poem he wrote, about a burning light, was so beautiful. I phoned friends immediately to inform them of this exciting new development in our relationship.

'It's Barry,' I said, 'he's here! He has finally got in touch outside of work.'

Friends were worried, I could tell in their voices.

'Has he, now?' asked one, with doubt in her voice. 'Has he phoned you?'

'Well not exactly, no.'

I knew she was going to find the next sentence bizarre but I trusted that, no matter what she felt or thought, she would not be cross with Barry. It never even entered my head that she might think it was all an illusion.

'No, it's not quite like that. He can't phone me, can he?' I told her in no uncertain terms. 'He's been banned from speaking to me, remember? And he isn't going to risk his job, is he?' I explained rather brusquely, feeling insulted that she couldn't read my mind and just know all these things. Going through it all again felt like wasting precious energy.
'He's built me two websites so that I can communicate with him. I guess he does it at work as well as at home. It's genius, it's pure genius,' I said.

'And how do they work then?' she enquired. She was starting to sound a little bit more on board with me now.

'Well, the first one was to find things out about me, like getting me to do loads of quizzes to determine what sort of person I am, questions about my personality traits, questions about my intelligence, you know that type of thing, an information-gathering thing, you know that type of thing.'

I knew she understood, she was smart and, deep down

inside, she knew Barry loved me. She continued to go along with it.

'Right, so Barry made you a website so that he can connect with you outside of work, yes?' she reiterated. Recapping was something Barry did quite a lot of, saying back what I had already said as if I was stupid.

'Yes, that's right, you have got it, that's exactly what he has done and there isn't only one website, there are two now, TickleDotCom and LovingYou.com.'

I could tell that she was tired. She had been supporting me for months on the phone. Unlike others, Dawn was calm with me and never challenged my beliefs. Her work as a psychiatric nurse meant that she was familiar with mental people and all that that brings, and she had a way of dealing with this situation that didn't make me feel scared to discuss things like this with her.

She would never say, 'I am really worried about you', as she knew that that would then make me not want to communicate with her. She knew it would have made me feel like I was affecting others, and I didn't want that. There were no answers in this situation and, no matter how many people were 'really worried about me', there was not a damn thing anyone could do to stop it. I was safe, in an odd sort of way and it was like a virus that would eventually pass through my system.

I phoned another friend who, after a few days, came round to see for himself.

'It's not Barry, Kathryn, these are all different people writing their own stuff,' he said, abrupt and insensitive.

Sensing my rejection of this statement he softened his voice and tried to take it down a notch.

'Look, they all have different names! How could this be Barry? Does he never sleep?'

He was being careful not to make me cry, as he could see I was visibly upset at this suggestion.

'Of course he sleeps sometimes! He will have prepared all the poetry in advance to send in the middle of the night as he knows I do not sleep and wouldn't want me to think he doesn't love me in the night as well as in the day.'

He looked bemused and didn't know what to say. I wasn't happy that he doubted me. It was unnerving and I needed him to leave immediately. He was getting in the way of my relationship with Barry. I knew he liked me, so I knew that this was his way of trying to break Barry and me up. I wasn't playing, and asked him to leave.

I was angry. Angry that Barry couldn't just come and take me. Why all of this? When was he coming to me in person? I didn't know how long I could play this game for, having to convince people that this was Barry and he did actually really, really love me. I needed him near me and it just wasn't happening. My amazing poetic verses continued, but it wasn't always sweetness and light.

RESPECT
by Mrs Very Angry

U are so fucking ME OFF NOW, ITS RAININ MEN IN SHEFFIELD AND i CAN LET MYSELF GET ABSOLUTELY SO FUCKING FUCKED ANYTIME I WANTYOU PRICK. SO WHY DONT YOU SORT THIS SHIT OUT AND COME AND GIVE ME ONE4 MEH COS ILL TELL YOU WHY, YOURE FUCKIG SCARED, SCARED OF LOVE AND COMMITMENT, SCARED OF ME, SCARED OF RISKS, THIS IS AN OFFICAL WARNING, IM ON A GANG BANG!!!!!!!!!!!!!!
Mr. no body, useless limp cock White

Some of the poems and stories that Barry wrote referred to other women, perhaps past loves that he needed to free himself of in order to give himself wholly to me. Whatever they meant it was certainly pissing me off, but the anger was always short lived. Each day my mood fluctuated; sometimes happy, sometimes angry and sometimes desperately sad. The poems continued, mostly completely unintelligible and spelt wrong, possibly something to do with the amount of alcohol that I was pouring down my neck and also the speed that I was writing.

NOT HAPPY
by unicorn person

U FUCKING PRICK YOU WANKER TART FACE UP YOURE BUM SHUT YOURE GOB, EFFORT OF A man, you lied to me and you said that u would be twqo hours oif ehich meamkes uki ljhjklljfuifuidgxfgy6dwjkuxe89r5n7

well guck you

And sometimes they were really odd.

all cum art once like an orcesrtra of angels
by unicorn.sausages.busbies@up youre arse please.com
jusnt cum and give irt rtoo moe Barruy, im no rtmessin now, uyou know when m
I hate you Barry
By Drew Pocket

Each time, the anger would pass and I would soon resume basking in Barry's love and devotion to me.

r u cuming or what?
by Drew Berryfields

you are my lovely husband to be so cum and take me, stop it

with youre wonder words and take me for realy, I am bequesthwe
to you
I am wholy youres
I may not read so well
or write so good
but I think you know
I am beautful just being me
come please I beg u kind sir
come take my soul and merge it with yorues
for it be internettwinnned anyway
the thing is can you the makeouthe, me happoyieth this
eveningethhhhe, by granting me the pleasure of youre company
ethhe. o kind sir, befire I die, with you beneath me, wondering for
ever more coulethhe have savethhhhhed me from this terrible
desitinym of hot pokers and huge cocks, could you have stopped
her form going out into the wildeness to be a gatecrasher on a
Monday night, to find the ugly one, will her night in shining aroma
come and save her. tonight before her next public showdown
that might involve the local funeral; directors esquire.

There were morning poems, lunch-time poems, evening
poems and night-time poems. In total there were over 492
poems for Barry in the space of just three weeks. I couldn't
understand why my poems were never voted poem of the day
or even voted for at all. Either would have been appreciated.

At 3am, the love story that I had been sat waiting for for
weeks, the one story that would confirm that Barry was
coming for me, arrived. In it, it said that I was his long-
distance lover, a secret that he had to keep for now but he was
going to come and get me and make me his bride. That our
parents shouldn't find out as our strict religious code was
preventing us from being together.

Ecstatic – and undeterred that Barry was forty-nine and
probably didn't have a mum or dad, and me only having a

mum, and neither of us being religious – nothing could have made me happier. The sonnets leapt from the page and filled my heart with glee. An all-night shop at Asda to find some new 'love music' was in order.

I drove there, careful not to crash the car. As I walked in the entrance, it was as if I had walked on stage, walked into a room where everyone was about to stand up and applaud me. The piano started rolling into tambourine shake, and 'Love is in the Air' started up loudly on the speakers.

The shop was almost empty apart from a few customers and several people filling shelves. Like in the *Full Monty*, everyone started to shake their bum.

I danced up the cereal aisle, shoulders tapping to one side, stepping in synchronicity. Spinning on my heels every few steps, I was in heaven. I knew that Barry had requested this song for me; this was our song! He was watching every move I made, guiding me with signs, speaking soft words to me through music, taking me to my destination, the music section.

I made my way up the escalator; the department was mostly closed apart from one woman unpacking boxes. She stood up straight and asked if I needed assistance. 'I don't imagine many people shop for music at 3am,' I said to her.

She nodded at me as if I was a nutter and continued with her packing. As I walked round the 'three for a tenner' aisle, in front of me on the floor lay the exact CD that I had had in mind: this was the sign I needed to convince me that this was not illusion. No insanity, this was a real sign that he was near: The Stylistics.

We didn't need to be together physically, we didn't need to speak on the phone and we didn't need to buy into the petty, standardized, one-dimensional relationships that other people happily settle for, we were truly connected both telepathically and spiritually. That night he wrote:

So come to me and you will see
How two halves can make a whole.
No longer will we be just half
Because now we share one soul.
By Barry Bee

The poems were good and kept me happy for a few moments but I was getting impatient; I knew I had to meet Barry face-to-face.

The guy I had been talking to on messenger had said in that first chat that his name was Ian and I had refused to believe it. He stood out from all the other sides of Barry. This was soft, supportive Barry. He let me shout abuse at him through the keyboard and never took offence, just like Barry had done on the phone. I liked this side of Barry the best: the accommodating Barry, Barry the submissive, reacting to Kathryn the oscillating albatross who fluctuated between sadomasochistic domination and docile subordination.

I had now bought a goldfish and called it Barry, renamed the cat Barry and had started to hang around in Barry's Bar on London Road. Everything was about Barry and everything was for Barry. It was time to find out whether the guy I had been chatting to online for over a month really was Barry. Ian had said he was a gardener at Chatsworth House and that he resided in a large stone built house in Buxton. Barry had clearly researched the local area to have this level of knowledge.

That night, he came online.

'Do you want to come to over?' I typed in the little blue box in the right-hand side corner of my screen. This was a massive disinhibited step forward.

'What, now?' he replied.

It was late, very late. It was summer time and I'd got the large pool that I had got myself arrested over only a few weeks earlier out on the lawn, full of water.

'I am ready to find out whether or not you are really Barry and I don't want to speak to you on the phone to find out, I couldn't handle that, I need to see your face.'

I had no idea what Barry looked like but felt sure this was him. I felt sure that he had come up to Sheffield for a few weeks to be near me and possibly rented a cottage in Derbyshire. I had had my doubts that it wasn't the real Barry but I had pushed them to the far corners of my mind.

Without too much thought or hesitation I said, 'Come over now, please, I need to meet you.'

For a few moments the box was empty, no 'in chatting mode' symbol appeared. I could sense that he was taking a deep breath. I knew that whoever this was had developed feelings for me that were quite strong. I had shared my stories with him and he had been on a journey with me, even if he wasn't Barry.

Text appeared in the box, a simple, 'OK.'

Suddenly a wild and tempestuous panic set in. It was late, and the thought did cross my mind that this might not be such a great idea, given that I didn't know this person at all. Other than chatting to him for over four weeks online I hadn't spoken to him or even seen a picture of him. I kind of thought about the fact that no one really knows anyone until they meet them, and that some people can live together for many years and still not know each other. There have been rapists whose wives have known nothing about it, and many people who have secret lives they keep from their loved ones. This justification of what I was about to do convinced me that it would be alright to let this person know where I live, that it was safe as long as it was on my terms. No coming into the house, we would sit in the garden and drink wine; civilised and safe.

He arrived at my home an hour later. I peeked out of the window to see a smart black Lexus car pull up behind my falling apart blue Nova. My car had been stolen and recovered so many times that I had stopped cleaning the writing on the window off that the police had written so it said, 'Scrap metal, no. 365745'. I just left it so they didn't have to bother the next time it got nicked.

My skip on wheels was in direct contrast to the car that was now parked behind it. It was hard to see his features from the window in the dark; it was nearly midnight. He was holding something in his hand, and I wondered whether it was large carving knife to stab me with. It was in a plastic Waitrose bag: he clearly had a taste for good food but so did Hannibal Lecter.

I greeted him at the back door. He was tall and quite handsome, and he handed me the bag, which had a bottle of wine in it.

'That's for you,' he said in a soft but undeniably Manchester accent. My heart sank to the depths of the ocean.

'You really aren't Barry, are you?' unable to conceal the disappointment in my voice. Tears ran down my cheeks. I felt sad and foolish all rolled into one.

'I am so sorry Kathryn, I did try and tell you I wasn't Barry but you just didn't want to hear it', he responded, placing his arms around me to comfort me. He was quite a large man and I sank into his embrace. For a moment, I felt secure and safe.

I invited him to sit down outside at the garden table. I'd lit candles all around the garden and had placed floating candles in the pool. We chatted until 2am when I decided it would be a good idea to lie in the pool and look at the stars. If he was going to kill me this would be his perfect opportunity, the drowning of Kathryn in her own fifteen-foot paddling pool…

Semi naked, we both climbed into the pool that had been warmed by the sunlight earlier in the day. It was still hot outside and the passions that burned within me matched the heat of the summer's night. Sexual excitement was at an all-time high, and I didn't know whether this was the symptom of the condition or not. But there was something liberating about being half naked in a pool with a man I had only just met in the middle of the night. It was wild but, as exciting as it was, I wasn't with Barry. Ian was a stand in, the body double, and he knew it. He knew I was never going to feel anything for him whilst Barry was on the scene.

The next day, hangover in hand, I looked under my bed and found bags upon bags filled with yet more writing. I didn't know where it was all coming from: it was clear it was all my work but I had no memory of writing any of it.

I was drowning in the writings and musings of a mad woman. Suffocating in sentences, submerged in adulation and up to my eyes in debt. I put my new CD into the PC and turned up the volume: The Stylistics, '7000 Dollars and You'.

Silly Poems = Mad Cow

ELEVEN

On a Mission

THE NOVA WAS ON ITS last legs. The driver door had been patched with tin foil and superglue. The steering lock had been completely smashed and was being held together with a mixture of toothpaste and chewing gum, and the exhaust wafted around like a sheet in the wind. It was a heap. But it was the only mode of transport I had and nothing was going to prevent me from finding my one true love, my soul mate: Barry White.

To make entirely sure that Barry knew that I was a woman of great interest and passion with a flair for romance, I sent him a trail of puzzles which would lead him to the Lakeside campsite in Oxford, where I had booked myself a space. I sent several campsites in the local area an envelope, each with a small key in – the key to my heart – each containing a clue of where to find me next. Each envelope was addressed for the attention of Mr Barry White. Inside it read 'Barry, well done for finding your first clue! Don't look for me here as there is more to come, look for the site beginning with…'

I had no idea why this was important but it was. I hoped he had enough petrol in his car as I had no idea how far away from each other these sites were. I figured that he would book the whole day off work and, if he started searching for me at 10am, then he should be with me by 5pm.

Lakeside campsite was enclosed and felt safe. It had two indoor swimming pools that were totally enclosed. I felt vulnerable and, although my normal camping preference was to stay on sites with minimal facilities, I thought that I would treat myself to a spot of five-star camping.

After a long drive, I arrived just in time to pitch the tent and get ready for Barry's big entrance. By my reckoning he would be here about 5.30ish. I wrote a postcard with the last clue on it:

Well done for finding me my true love,
You've managed to navigate to the last clue.
Look for the tent, it is blue
I'll be waiting for my love for you is true,
Oh just to add, I am five foot nine, medium build, smiley face
with a bit of a bobbly nose, blonde hair and have jeans and a
red top on.

I left it on reception and returned to my tent.

I laid out some Scotch eggs on two paper plates and placed the wine in the cool bag. I straightened the rug I had bought in Ikea, along with two new large wine glasses and a lucky bamboo stick.

I got the lighthouse out of the car, the one I had bought in the antique shop weeks earlier. I put it in the tent, with a note stuck to it for Barry telling him to go to the big pool. I'd wrapped the lighthouse carefully in brown paper, just in case he peeped inside; I didn't want to spoil the surprise.

Five o'clock came, and there was no sign of Barry. I wasn't worried because I knew that he loved me and there was no way on this earth that he was going to let me down.

I had no idea why I thought it important that on our first meeting I should be swimming and him watching but it was. *How will I know who he is?* I wondered to myself. *Perhaps I will just know because he will be the only clothed person in there.* I got ready for the pool and walked to the reception.

The pool was clean and fresh looking, as if it had just been built. The ceiling was arched and covered in wood panelling like a Swedish cabin. It had a sauna, a steam room and a Jacuzzi. Giddy and full of trepidation I kept dropping the things that I was trying to hold, first the pen then the flip-flops. I bent down to gather my belongings and a whirling sensation hit me.

Steadying myself with my hand on a display cabinet, I made my way to the pool area. There were two pools: a large, rectangular-shaped pool on one side of the building and a smaller, kidney-shaped pool with soft lighting and a lagoon feel to it.

Feeling wobbly, I lowered myself into the water. How excited I felt. This was it! This was going to be the greatest love affair of all time. The scene was set, the music was perfect, the ambience just right. Back and forth I swam in time, always keeping my eye on the door. I felt sick with nerves.

An hour passed and my heart began to sink. Deep down inside I knew he wasn't coming. My neck started to become stiff from the constant watching of the entrance door. I was bored and upset and needed to get out. I sat in the sauna to contemplate my next move

A couple were perched on the high bench to the left. They were young and were laughing and smiling at each other, sharing a private moment. They said hello to me and I returned the gesture. After the polite greetings – I don't quite know how – Barry cropped up in the conversation. I knew my mouth was running away with me like a high-speed train without the brakes. Faster and faster I sped through a very intense, but nonetheless packed version of the last three months. It felt like I needed to share everything with them about my private life as if I was in a very hot confession box. Before I knew where I was I blurted out…

'Oh yes, I make Barry laugh alright, like the time when I was talking too much and I shouted down the phone, "Barry White why don't you just come up to Sheffield and shove your big fat fucking cock in mouth to shut me up?"'

They looked at each other, picked their towels up and rapidly left the sauna. I felt exposed.

Doubt started to set in. I couldn't understand why Barry wasn't here. I kept telling myself over and over, *he will be here and there must be a really good reason why he isn't like he's shampooing orphaned kittens or has suddenly been chosen for game show and has been whisked off by ITV. After all why wouldn't he come?*

Deep down I knew the real reason he couldn't come, and that was because 'they' were preventing him. There were two things that I had never considered in all of this: what Barry looked like, and whether he was married or not. Both seemed trivial details in that moment. I got back into the water and swam.

Eventually, I gave up before I shrivelled like a prune or drowned. I got dried and dressed and returned to the tent; it was starting to go dark. I wanted to go for a walk and explore that area to clear my head but I was anxious in case he arrived when I was gone. I put my hands together and lowered my head to pray to whoever would listen; God the Universe, I didn't care.

My prayer was simple and slightly resembled the lyrics from an Oleta Adams song: 'Barry, I don't care how you get here, just get here when you can.'

Eight o'clock arrived, and still no sign of Barry. I paced up and down my eight foot square piece of land I had rented for two days, itching to call his office. I wished I didn't have to go through reception to get to 'him'. I knew that they all thought that I was a nutter and that all this was really funny and I didn't want to have to deal with their attitude but I so needed to speak with him.

Nine o'clock arrived, and still no Barry. I decided that I would go ahead with tea without him. I carefully laid out two plates and put Barry's dinner out for him, covering his scotch egg with cling film.

I opened the wine.

I rolled a cigarette.

Ten o'clock arrived; still no Barry. I couldn't hold out any longer. I dialled the number carefully on my mobile, knowing it off by heart now. One of the intake counsellors answered the phone.

'I need to speak with Barry please, it's Drew Berryfields,' I said in my pseudo-intellectual accent.

Changing my name to try and get through to Barry was something I had started since they had terminated all contact with him. No matter what skill I put into disguising my voice, they knew it was me. The man on the other end told me that Barry was not in the office and that if I wanted to speak with another counsellor I could. I declined the offer and asked him to leave a message for Barry:

'Phone me, you fucking blockhead, because if you don't I'm gonna shout and scream until I get myself arrested and I will tell everyone what a crap therapist you really are. Hell hath no fury like a woman scorned, Barry.'

Ten minutes later the phone rang. It was Barry.

'Hello you,' his soft voice echoed around my head.

Still getting to grips with the fact that he was on the phone and not in my tent with me, wrapped up all warm and snuggling, singing sweet songs into my ear, I responded, 'Barry, why aren't you here?'

'You know I can't answer that,' he politely replied.

'Well actually, I think that after I've gone to all this trouble to get here and buy you a nice tea and everything, I think that at least I deserve to know whether you wanted to come here or not.' I took a breath. 'If you didn't want to come then fine, fuck off, but just tell me Barry, did you want to come?'

I was sure that everyone in the other tents could hear this as it had gone eerily silent.

'It's hard,' Barry replied.

'What's hard Barry, your cock?'

Barry laughed. His laugh was laced with sadness; sadness because there was little he could do to help. He knew I was in danger and out there all alone, and he knew no one was really bothered about what was happening to me and that I was extremely mentally unwell.

'Listen, I need to speak with you.'

I knew what was coming and I couldn't handle it, not now, not here. This was way too messy and one wrong word could be so detrimental.

'Don't, Barry, please don't say it. I know what you are going to say and I don't want to hear it, not now. I'm in a terrible state and I'm alone on this campsite in the middle of a place I don't know and I feel very vulnerable.'

Barry agreed not to say it. There was a silent pause on the phone, I breathed in through my nose, absorbing his love from afar, trying to capture these seconds of having him with me in our own little world of telephone love.

'There is the little matter of what I should do with this gift that I have bought for you, though. The way that I see it is that I can either throw it in the Thames and you can catch it as it reaches Oxford centre, or I can leave it at the St Aldgate's church for you to collect at your leisure. Or I could give it away,' I said.

'Why don't you just hang onto it for now?' Barry suggested.

My tummy started to do somersaults. That was it! I knew that he had feelings for me, he must do or else he wouldn't have asked me to keep hold of it. I told Barry that this was to be the last time that I would contact him and that I needed to sort myself out. I said goodbye and switched the phone off.

The night was cold and, because I had believed that Barry was going to come to me, I hadn't brought enough covers, so I spent most of the night in the toilet block keeping warm under the hand dryer. They had nice music in the toilets.

The next morning I felt shocking, having necked two bottles of red wine and spending most of the night writing some shit or other, drawing comparisons between myself and Mozart. I was determined to get to the Mary Virgin church. The mother of all churches; my vehicle to the big guy.

I caught the bus into Oxford on the park and ride, which was an enormous achievement given the state that I was in. It didn't take long before I reached the church but, just as I walked into the front entrance, I tripped. My sandal broke and the hipster trousers that I knew were getting too big for me because I hadn't been eating and taking care of myself properly, fell to my knees. With the help of a passer-by I picked myself up and walked bare foot through Oxford to purchase some new sandals.

I returned to the church and went inside. It was smaller and darker than I had imagined, with statues of all the saints carved into the walls. Apart from the sound of footsteps, the rustling of plastic carriers and the clicks of the cameras, it was silent, silent and deeply moving. I sat on a chair and, with my hand on my heart, I said a little prayer asking to be shown in the right direction, praying for a sign that he was near me. I needed to make sure I had covered all bases here with God, given that I had never been bought into the idea that we had been created by God, but this was a serious situation and I needed some serious help. I did my best to make it up to him just in case he did in fact exist. Just to make sure I had been properly heard, I shimmied over to the notice board, pushing everyone out of the way and placed a little note for Barry.

'Barry White, get your big fat arse over here and help me out' I wrote. Tears ran down my face. I felt sad and alone.

I walked down Aldgate Road. This was meant to be the perfect weekend and it was ruined. I had a sensation within me to be as open as I could possibly be to new experiences and follow whatever sign was put in front of me and right in front of me was a sign outside another church, this time a very different looking church, a new build, an evangelical church, saying that there was a free art exhibition on today.

Being a free spirit, I entered the church. Three tables were in the entrance all selling crafts and art work. I briefly looked at them before entering the main part of the church. The pictures, photos and sculptures had all been created by parishioners and had a religious theme. One of them particularly stood out and was titled, 'God put Adam to sleep in order to create Eve', by the artist Sharon Wiper. I knew in that moment I was in the right place and that out of despair, out of darkness and sadness something beautiful was going to be born.

Barry had walked here. I could feel his footsteps before me, his scent lingering in the air. He had left a trail of calm and peace to wrap around me and in that moment, the anxiety lifted and was replaced by an overwhelming sense of enlightenment.

Sitting at one of the tables in the foyer, an older lady chatted quietly to a younger female. I looked at her stall and all the tiny painted glass pieces she had made herself and was selling. I was drawn to a small boat painted in red, yellow and blue on which it was sailing on a rough sea. 'You like that one don't you,' she said. I hadn't even picked the piece up and she knew exactly which one I was drawn to.

'Yes I do, it's how I feel at the moment, like a boat lost at sea on a turbulent tide, not knowing if I will make it back to shore, not knowing if I want to make it back to shore.' She picked the piece up, walked around the table and, holding my hand, she pressed the small glass boat into my palm.

I began to cry uncontrollably. I hadn't cried like this for a long time. The grief came from the pit of my stomach, grief that had been stored away.

Holding me close, she took my hand and led me into the main part of the chapel. Standing behind me she placed both her hands heavy upon my shoulders, bowing her head so it rested on my back. No words were spoken or exchanged. I knew she had been waiting for me to come to her. She had been placed there on that stall on that day, selling her glass trinkets to draw me to her. 'There will be a service here tomorrow, I may or may not be here but you should try your best to come.' That was my second sign.

With that, she looked into my eyes like an old friend, smiled, let go of my hands and returned to her stall. I went over to pay her for the glass boat. She raised her hand in a gesture to say she didn't want money for it. I smiled at her and left. She had seen my soul.

I thought of the lighthouse as I left the church holding the boat in the palm of my hand. It was all coming together. Barry coming to the campsite was too easy. He wanted a bigger, better entrance into my life. He wanted the whole wide world to know just how much he loved me. I needed to be patient. The seed had been sown, like a child in the womb, there was nothing more I could do to bring him to me but wait. Patience had never been my strong point.

That night I was restless. A small child in the tent next to mine had cried all night long. The parents weren't responding and for a moment I wondered if they had left the child alone. I wanted to intervene, to find out what was happening. I hated knowing a child was in distress. I tried to shut it out as I didn't know if I was reading the situation right and also I needed a break from my social work duties. It's like one of those professions where you are never off duty but this time I had to shut down for my own sake. I pulled the covers over my head and tried hard to ignore the situation.

The following morning I went for a swim early and then drove my car, with my lighthouse on the back seat, to the park and ride. With no sleep again and my nerves raw, I boarded the bus clutching the lighthouse which I had unwrapped, displaying all its beautiful, rich primary colours. As I sat down, lighthouse on the seat next to me, I reached into my pocket to be sure I had remembered the glass boat. I had paid special effort to my hair and had a sunny, short flowery dress on with small-heeled sparkly shoes.

The church was packed, which was not what I had expected at all. There were large screens both inside and out, with close ups of the preacher who was confident and charismatic. I was late and the service had started. I squeezed past every one. 'Excuse me, lighthouse coming through,' I said, as I rammed my way through the entrance to get to the main hub of the church. Only a few seats remained at the back and someone shuffled up a seat so both me and my lighthouse could both sit next to each other. I didn't know what was to come next or how this was going to play itself out. *Should I let someone know I am here?* I thought to myself. I guessed that they would already know that I had arrived as I was connected on a much higher spiritual level than anyone else in the church.

I waited patiently whilst several baptisms took place. The young people, no older than nineteen, one by one came to the stage and told their stories. The stories seemed to follow a pattern of abandonment, bullying, drug abuse, prostitution and then being saved by Jesus in various different combinations. Despite being psychotically very unwell and somewhat deluded myself, I still found it hard to believe the authenticity of the 'being saved by the hand of God' bit of this.

I hoped for them it was true and that their lives had improved since allowing Jesus in. I felt sad that I lived in a society where there were few other places people in distress could get help from, after all, I also stood in this space with them.

After the baptisms were over, my legs got twitchy, *Is it now?* I kept thinking to myself, *Is this the time when something will happen?* I couldn't bear the thought of the service ending and nothing had happened and I feared that there was a small chance that this could indeed happen.

The preacher said a few more words about God and then he asked if there was anyone in the audience that wanted to speak with God. I knew this was my invite onto that stage. This was the moment I had been waiting for. I had to let Barry know I was here in this audience for him to come and take me and show me his undying love.

I quickly gathered up my lighthouse tucking it firmly under my arm and made my way to the front of the stage. The lighthouse, which was made of resin, was light to carry. People looked at each other and I could hear giggles and whispers as I made my way to the front of the stage but I didn't care because they didn't have what I had. I had Barry and we had the whole world looking at our beautiful love affair. Swiftly moving as if being transported on a travellator escalator in an airport, I glided past all the other people who seemed to be gathering speed as if there was a rush on bread at the local supermarket. I wanted to be first. The silver haired charismatic pastor was bending down from the stage to acknowledge them as they huddled together like a flock of sheep waiting to board the all-singing and all-dancing locomotion to salvation.

He looked up and saw me, standing there with a white glow of light emanating from my body and my lighthouse. He beckoned me to him on stage. I knew in my soul that, at this exact time in this exact space there was a greater force working its magic: this was the end of my journey, the place where I would fall into Barry's safe arms forever. I knew he was in this room; he was here for me. Of that I was sure.

He held out his oversized hairy hands and gently guided me up the stairs as if it were all part of the show. Whilst keeping hold of my hand, he presented me to the congregation. Hundreds and hundreds of people were gathered right before my eyes and I knew they were all there for me, waiting in eager anticipation to what I had to say. The spot light shifted from the pastor onto me and I was there, and they were waiting. Waiting for something to come out of my mouth, but I had no idea what that something was going to be.

'Tell us all who you are my dear,' my legs wobbled as he passed me the microphone.

'Er, my name is Kathryn,' I muttered barely audible into the heavy silver wand with a large furry ball on top.

'And where do you come from Kathryn?'

I hesitated, knowing that as soon as I said where I was from they would all know it was me. 'I'm from Sheffield.' A few people in the crowd to the left of me shout 'yeah!' signalling that they were from my hometown.

'And what have you come to say Kathryn?' Momentarily, I stood in silence, staring into the crowd, taking in the enormity of this overwhelming situation.

'He loves me,' I proclaimed. 'I know he loves me.'

'He loves her!' the charismatic pastor shouted as he retrieved the microphone from me. 'Tell us more about this amazing being that loves you so very much, Kathryn,' he said.

Silence fell like a blanket across the congregation, my voice becoming louder and more confident with each sentence.

'He is here with me, right here, right now!' I shouted, grinning like a Cheshire cat.

'Hallelujah!' several people shouted.

'Praise the Lord! He's here with you!' a random person shouted back at me.

'He is in this room right now, I know he is, I can feel him, I can sense his presence but I cannot see him.' More people shouted 'Hallelujah praise the lord!' One woman shouted in an American accent, 'You'd better believe it gal.' With this approval, I continued.

'He speaks to me all the time, guiding me, protecting me and he told me to come here, through a woman I met yesterday. I knew this was the place he would be waiting for me!'

People began to rising to their feet, chanting, 'Hallelujah, praise the lord, he loves you,' I continued.

'I knew he wouldn't let me down, he never lets me down, not on purpose.'

'Praise the Lord, he is within you!' someone else shouted back at me. This was all going swimmingly well, I thought.

'Yes, I know he is within me; he's in my head, and he is in my soup!' *He's in my soup! Where the hell did that come from?* I thought to myself.

'He's with me every day! He lies with me at night, speaks to me when I am scared and holds my hand when I'm shopping in Asda!'

Everyone was on their feet; they really liked the Asda bit. I was really getting into the swing of this!

'No matter how many people try and take me down, he'll be there to save me; he will keep me alive on this planet!'

I started to feel a bit panicky as I was running out of things to say and Barry was supposed to have stepped forward out of the crowd by now. He had got all these people here for me, this was the greatest love of all time but the second main star of the show was missing. I wondered if I would recognise him but realised that of course I would; he would be surrounded by a glowing light, not as bright as my own glowing light of course, but his light would be so strong he would fill my heart the moment I saw him.

'I love him and he loves me. I know he loves me!' I shouted loud and theatrically, and then I said it, 'Barry White, reveal yourself to me now!' I love you Barry White.'

The room fell silent and people began to sit down, hands around their mouths, shocked and trying not to laugh at me.

My voice became weaker, more vulnerable, 'Barry, reveal yourself to me now, please, I know it's you! You made this happen; I know you love me!'

This was now starting to look like a Greek tragedy. It was not supposed to be this way; this was not the scene I had in mind.

The kind people crowded round me, overpowering me with their presence on the stage, too many people speaking all at once, too much commotion, too much noise. Confused and bewildered, I was ushered off the stage.

There was no Barry in the room; there was no telepathy. I was not only mental; I was insane.

Nicky and Nigel Woolleyhouse had been in the congregation. They were devout Christians and lived near St Aldgates in Oxford. Many people were trying to talk to me and make sure I was safe, but they could see I wasn't coping and dragged me to one side. They pulled their car round to the back of the church and huddled me and my lighthouse in.

I felt frightened and exposed as they welcomed me into their home. They made me a drink and took me to sit by a river that ran through their back garden. They were a married couple who rented a flat in Oxford. They had no children and I sensed that their own deep sadness was born from this travesty. Here I was, deeply traumatised, picnicking next to a little stream like something from *The Waltons*, on the lawn of complete strangers' house in a place where I had never been and yet it felt OK. It felt as if it was indeed the place where I needed to be most in the world, right in that moment.

This divine intervention was most welcome. Their faith

was clear and somewhere between the olives and tortillas and the cheese and pickle sandwiches, Jesus joined us. They had faith and I admired that. I wished that I, too, could have believed in something as strongly as they did. But other than Barry, I didn't. We had been to church as children, all immaculately dressed, shoes polished, hair combed and tied back, disabled father in tow. I had become disillusioned by the whole faith thing at an early age when our own Methodist church had failed to do little to support our family other than to turn up and play the brass band directly outside our front window on Christmas Eve, something Mum hated as it singled us out as being a 'family in need'. I also had an innate distrust for vicars. I had no problem with other people believing but it wasn't for me and, despite my recent courting with madness and the idea of a strong spiritual connection with Barry, I preferred fact. We exchanged hugs and I left, to return to my little tent in the middle of nowhere.

I poured myself the last of the wine and sat on my rug contemplating what to do next. A woman walked past.

'May I join you?' she asked, whilst peering round and inside my tent.

'Winter will soon be upon us,' she added in a voice that felt like it was saying, 'I am nice really, I'm not a bad person, look see I can talk about the weather, this makes me completely harmless!'

I beckoned her towards me and invited her to share the last of my bottles of wine. I'd already had enough to sink a ship.

We quickly established the facts: I was here because I was mad, and she was here because she was mad in an un-mad way. Judith had a husband, and she explained that things had become rather dull in their marriage. She had felt, after having four children and giving him twenty years of sexual favours, washing, cooking and ironing, her time had come to live a little. Her rebirth had come in the shape of a nineteen-year-old born-again Christian by the name of Ryan who was sleeping in the tent three doors away from me. Judith had committed adultery.

'Do you think it's wrong for a forty-seven-year-old woman to be cavorting with a nineteen-year-old boy? That's what he is really, isn't it, a boy?'

It felt weird that a stranger was seeking my approval in the middle of nowhere on the grass.

'He makes me feel special, young and free,' she continued.

I didn't doubt that, I had heard the evidence of it the night before. The more she talked about his fulfilling her desires, the more shit I felt. Where was my fun? Where was my Barry?

She continued. 'All of the things my boring husband stopped doing six months after we met, the last nineteen and a half years have been... well anyway, Ryan excites me.' There was really little need to justify herself to me, I was not in the least bit judgmental about such things.

She looked around, as if needing some approval from someone, the night sky even.

'So, is it wrong do you think?' she asked again.

She knew the answer really, we all know the answers to our problems but usually we just don't like admitting we know and we don't trust our inner thoughts enough. The truth is hard, and facing reality is hard.

'Yes, I think it's, well, it's odd, but there again, there aren't many things that are even stranger and probably morally and ethically much worse than what's happening in your life my dear, so I'm probably not the best person to ask.'

She looked at me, startled.

'Odd, what do you mean odd?' she asked, cocking her head slightly as if she was getting water out of her ear.

I continued, 'Yes, it's odd. Religion, that is. I don't understand how people can worship something their whole lives that only has a very slim chance of actually existing. That's what I don't get. However,' I continued, 'I'm not exactly far from that myself.'

'OK, so taking aside the Christian thing, do you think I'm bad for having an affair?' I wished we could have just swapped lives just for one week or one year. I wish she could have played the part of the 'nutter' and I 'the adulterer'. I would rather be that than be this.

In that moment, on that day, in that space, we were two different people from completely different worlds but we had similar problems. We both bore the scars and wounds of motherhood and we both shared a deep sense of loss and loneliness. We both had plenty of people in our lives, yet we were both lost, desperate for something that was not there, living in a fantasy world. She was doing marginally better than I was, though, because at least she was having sex. All I had stashed away in my tent was some Scotch eggs and a three-foot lighthouse.

TWELVE

What Goes Up Must Come Down
October 2004

IN 1929, KARINTHY'S THEORY OF 'chain links' suggested that with the growing emergence of technological advancement in communication and friendship, we were all connected to each other by only five acquaintances. In 2006, Facebook claimed that six degrees of separation had now become four but in 2004, I proved that the chain link has been reduced further to two. For, on 8th October 2004, three people would witness events that would not only remain with them for the rest of their lives, but also had a connection in some way to their own lives. These three complete strangers who happened to be in the same place at the exact same time witnessed a horrific incident that they would later share with their friends and their loved ones. It turned out that the people they told were people in my own friendship circle. But not one of these people would ever have known, at that point, that it was me that was lying on the concrete on that bleak, rainy autumn day.

It's hard to put an exact time on when my mood shifted from being high to permanently low. The high had been alarming but the low turned out to be much more disturbing. Unfortunately for all bipolar sufferers, what goes up must come down and I was no exception. I trawled the internet for information on what to expect from the illness and, upon finding a site that explained the illness really well, I started to think that maybe I did have the condition.

I knew that there had been a book written by Kaye Redfield Jamison about her own experiences of being bipolar but my community psychiatric nurse had warned me off reading it due to my low mood. I needed something, though, some explanation as to why all these things were happening to me, an explanation of how the mind works and – more importantly – strategies for dealing with this shift in mood. Previously, I had had a mixture of feelings of severe elation and depression but something had changed.

Catatonic and morose, I became uncommunicative and withdrawn. The writing had ceased and been replaced by a growing fear of the outside world, along with a belief that I was no longer a part of this society. I was an outcast, a fraudulent human. I popped my pills in the desperate hope that they would kick in and transform me into my former self. They had stopped the mania, the anxiety and the irritability but it had been replaced by something more horrific and unnerving. What had happened before had been a real cocktail of emotions tearing their way through my world like a twister, picking up debris and throwing it around, bashing its way through my life, ruining everything I had ever achieved by making me a laughing stock and an object of ridicule. But now I was being drawn into the black hole at the epicentre of my illness, negativity clinging to my soul like a magnet picking up pins, whirling around destroying everything in its path.

Each morning, I could think of nothing to do except sit and stare at blank walls. I had repainted the room three times in the last few months: first to cover up the writing, then to make it look as if I were at the seaside and, more recently, black. A total blackout. There seemed no point in anything.

Why wash when I am going to die eventually? Why bother

brushing my teeth or getting dressed? If I get dressed I will have to get dressed every morning, every morning would be the same. Washed, dressed, teeth cleaned, breakfast, work, home, wash, undressed, teeth cleaned, bed and so on.

The repetitive monotony of these daily chores seemed so utterly pointless. Life seemed utterly pointless. I questioned why people went to the effort of learning new skills when, at any given moment, their lives could end. I had had a mini version of this since being a child. Overwhelmed by the amount of things to learn about the world, I shut down to learning anything other than what would get me through lessons without looking a twit.

There were things that needed doing. The house needed a good clean: it looked like the Marie Celeste, and hadn't been cleaned properly for months at that stage. I simply couldn't bear to do it, the same thoughts about repetitiveness prevailed.

Why bother? It will only need doing again next week and the week after. The dreariness of this dull existence felt so very real. For years I'd cut the hedge, mowed the grass of not only my own house but the two elderly neighbours both next door and at number 8. As soon as I'd finished one, the other needed doing again. It was the same with the car, the house, the litter tray, the decorating, our hair, our nails, everything. Repeat, repeat, repeat.

Everything seemed so unbelievably heavy and hard work, like driving a car without power steering after having the luxury of having one with it. There was no end to it. Was that the point of life, a constant replay of events?

Ian remained a constant in my life, checking in on me every day either by phone or messaging. He, like Barry had been close enough to me to see the changes from high to low and now to very low. Increasingly concerned about my suicidal ideation, he demanded to see or hear from me at least once a week. We arranged to meet in a village in Derbyshire, near to where he lived. Sitting in his car for hours, not speaking, head bowed, I realised that this situation was serious. He didn't object to suicide being the only topic of conversation, but I could see the anguish on his face and feel his helplessness. He had loved and lost before, that was clear. His former partner had been a drug user. She had borrowed money from him one night and the next day was found in bed, alone, dead from a drug overdose. Her drug debt had plunged him into a serious financial situation and he carried the cross of guilt for being the one who had given her the tools to die.

As gentle and as kind as he was, he could not have single-handedly fixed her and he knew he could not fix me. I could see in his eyes that he was looking for the rewind button, to replay and resolve his own painful past. I wondered if, by saving me, he could pay back into the bank of karma, but he was out of his depth and he knew it.

As the days and weeks passed, I completely stopped being able to care for myself in any way. I sat and stared and sat and stared. Mum would cook a dinner for me and I would just stare at it. I was not hungry; I was not anything. I had no feelings other than an increasingly strong desire to die.

Day and night, I stared at the walls. I watched every painful minute pass on the clock. The clock in the kitchen was out of synch with the one in my room, so for every second there was an extra one, making the situation even more unbearable. I counted the hours down until the day was over and then it would all start up again, more of the same. Barry was gone, and I no longer cared. Barry this and Barry that. It had all been a dream, an illusion and me, well, I had been a stupid fool.

The realisation that Barry was not real made me feel worse. He was real in the sense that he existed and he was real in the sense that he had been in my life as a professional but he wasn't the Barry I wanted him to be. Real people interact with you on a fairly regular basis; you have physical contact with real people. I didn't even know what Barry looked like; I knew nothing about him, nothing at all. I had booked a church and told everyone that Barry was going to marry me, and I felt deeply embarrassed about it. People would now see me as the village idiot, the nutter that can't get a bloke so she books the church, orders his suit and then finds a guy to slot straight into it. I had lined up all my bridesmaids – twelve very concerned friends – and I had bought a wedding dress at a total cost of £2,500. And now nothing.

All the dreams and the plans came to nothing because none of it was real. I didn't know why I had created this fantasy and I did not know why Barry was the chosen one. Reality was calling and I wasn't ready for it. It felt harsh and serious and I wasn't well enough to deal with any of it, I couldn't deal with life.

Lost and alone, detached from everyone, devoid of all normal human emotion, I sat and I waited. It was black or white, no in-between, no compromise. Live or die.

Work hadn't been in touch for months, and that unnerved me. I had thought about taking Faye with me, to die. I loved her so much and I knew there was nobody on this entire planet that I would trust to look after her. I knew what children's homes were like and I wouldn't put a dog in most of them, never mind a child. There were some really good foster carers but, for every good one there was also bad, and Mum couldn't have coped: they were like chalk and cheese.

Serious consideration of the care options for my child after my death seemed somewhat normal; this was a point of no return. I'd lost all faith in the mental health team and couldn't understand why these people were getting paid for seemingly doing absolutely nothing. I thought about all the good, creative things that could be done with just the salary of one psychiatrist. I could have Googled my symptoms and come up with the same diagnosis as they had. What was of more concern to me right now was that I had struck a deal with the devil: it was just a matter of how I did this and whether or not Faye would be part of the deal.

I had asked for social work input to help me sort through things, but it was not forthcoming. They had sent a colleague round when I first expressed intentions of suicide some months before and I had explained that I had considered taking Faye with me. I never saw anyone again.

I had a deep sense of paranoia about work which had been exacerbated by the lack of dialogue and support from them. I had never expected to go into social work believing that I would at some stage need social work support, though it didn't surprise me. I'd worked on a similar case myself and had been forced to pull out as social services had felt it was the mental health team's responsibility, and while the buck gets passed around, the situation on the ground becomes more and more explosive.

I thought about the enquiries that had taken place after incidents like this, and how easy it is to fudge the truth of failure, to rewrite case notes, rewrite events, how to turn bad practice into good. I wondered whether there would be a review after I had gone. Points for practice that get adopted for the first few months after an event and then pushed to one side, boxed up and forgotten about; paperwork gathering dust on a tall shelf somewhere that no one ever looks at. What I didn't understand is how they could leave one of 'their own' so out in the cold.

I'd watch people with jealousy in my eyes, wishing I could be them. I would have gladly swapped my brain with someone else's just to be able to think and feel and love again, to have a workplace, to communicate and to laugh. More than anything I missed laughing. Nothing seemed funny anymore, but nothing seemed sad either, there was simply a dark, dull void, an unnerving emptiness.

Faye was getting worse and I didn't know how to deal with the situation. I tried to block out the pain of knowing how unhappy she really was, with no idea of how to deal with it.

She was starting to place herself in risky situations, drinking more with her mates, smoking weed and getting involved with not only boys, but men. Her friends seemed to grow more and more aggressive, angry and mutinous. I didn't want them near the house, I felt unsafe with them around and I didn't want them to see me like this. Like vultures sensing death, they came and they made me afraid. I had once been so strong and fun to be around and now I was a mess.

As the weeks passed, I did less and less. I desperately wanted to be with friends but could not talk. I constantly worried that I was a drain on everyone around me and had taken to my bed as it seemed the only safe place to be during this terrible malaise. The hardest thing of all was trying to keep communicating with Faye. I was getting scared for her mental health; I knew I was making her ill and the more I worried about it, the harder it was to be the person she so needed and deserved.

'I just want my mum back, where have you gone?' Faye asked, repeatedly.

I saw my CPN on a weekly basis and I was getting less and less out if it. We didn't connect in any way, and I had lost all faith that there was anyone out there that could actually connect with me or understand this malady. No appointment with a counsellor was forthcoming, despite it now being several months since this situation had begun. I was being fobbed off by an inadequate psychiatrist who spent little more than ten minutes every four weeks with me, and only ever to 'tweak' my medication. There was never a mention of counselling for myself or my child; just 40mg Citralopram and 10mg Olanzapine. I didn't want any more drugs! I wanted to talk with someone, someone who was really listening to me. Someone who showed some interest in my experience, who could help me to make some sense of what was happening and what had happened, not just in my past but my time as a social worker.

It was around this time that I finally plucked up the courage to have a look, for the first time in months, at my bank balance. I was fairly confident that there was plenty of money in there, and I remember going to the cash machine and my legs buckling under me. A nausea started at the base of my stomach and rose up into my throat as I looked at the balance: there had been £48,000 in April and there was a total of £300 left. I was gutted.

My friend Ralph had also become severely depressed and we briefly reconnected through this difficult time. We talked about suicide regularly, both methods and consequences, with deadly nightshade being high up on the list of possibilities. Suicide was all I wanted to talk about, because there was nothing else happening in my head. In the same way that the project, Barry, and the writing of the book had become my obsessions, so too had the idea of death. The taste of death was on my tongue and I wanted urgently to swallow it whole.

I had started to talk to my mum about the situation. I had managed to keep the full extent of my illness from her until then; I was concerned that she would consider me weak, as her expectations of humans had always been so high. Emotions were a sign of weakness in our family and I was definitely hit with the 'soft as shit stick' when I popped into the world. She was such a strong character, someone who had lived through many traumas and carried on regardless, that I felt ashamed that I wasn't coping and that everything had gone so badly wrong. For many months, I had played a game of avoidance to try and protect her and myself from negative and unhelpful comments, but to my surprise she was both supportive and empathetic. It became such that, night after night, I would drive up to her house and sit with her, crying and asking constantly if she loved me.

Mum believed that I was ill because I was lonely, so she tried her best to get me in touch with other people. I didn't know what I believed anymore and was willing to give anything a try to stay on the planet for one more day. She scanned the newspapers for lonely hearts clubs and arranged for me to go to a singles' night she'd seen an advert for. I really didn't want to go, it was far too much effort and the last thing I wanted to do was meet other desperados, other people who no one wanted to be around. But despite my reservations, and to make her happy, I went along.

It was held in a room above a run-down old pub in Hillsborough. I walked in and just stood there, looking at the sad situation.

'Are you a new member?' a man asked

'No, I don't think I am. I don't think I should be here, it's really not a place for me,' I stammered, trying carefully not to offend.

'We're all one big family 'ere you know, love,' he said in a broad Yorkshire accent. The word 'love' is an affectionate term used in these parts in nearly every exchange, and I liked that. He was a larger-than-average guy with a shiny red face and a grey, receding hairline, beckoning me to come closer. I could smell the familiar smell of BRUT aftershave on him, the 'in' smell of the 70's younger man.

'Come on in and give it a try, there are lots of women that come here, you might meet some new friends.' I didn't need new friends, more people to upset when I finally killed myself. I just needed to die.

I wanted the ground to open up and swallow me. Was this what I had been reduced to, a lonely hearts club? The 'disco depresso' of the universe? I didn't mind meeting people if they were prepared to talk all night about methods of suicide with me, but that was the only conversation I wanted with anyone. Several small round tables sat, empty, around the tiny dance floor, and a group of women in their mid-fifties who had taken up residence in the corner of the room were waving at me to join them. I paid my £1.50 entrance fee and walked into the desolate space.

There were a few older men dotted around the room, each occupying a separate table, glaring into their pint pots. I felt ridiculous being there. Although pulling men had never been a problem for me, I couldn't ever imagine anyone wanting a relationship with me now, not in this catatonic state. The only person I wanted to date was a Harold Shipman type. I looked around the room to see if I could see a serial killer who might want to date me. I would have been his dream girl, someone who wants to die. It would be a suicide that was also a murder. A murder would evoke sympathy, and it would be less hassle for me. The insurance would pay out on a murder. I pondered whether if I did put myself in that situation would I indeed be scared when the time came?

For a moment I was lost in my own thoughts. 'Is this your first time, love?' one of the women asked. 'You don't need to be shy, we are all really nice here and we will look after you.'

'How old are you, love?' another woman asked, 'You only look like a baby.'

I cleared my throat. 'I am thirty-four,' I replied.

'Oh, you are young!' she looked round the table at her pals. 'Isn't she young?'

I didn't like this place one bit; it was like a cattle market. I made up a story, saying that I had been married and my husband had run off with my best friend and this was my first time out of the house.

They looked at each other and as if synchronised they all said 'Bastard!' at the same time whilst nodding in disapproval to each other.

'They're all bastards love,' another added.

This prompted an outpouring of their own stories of the 'bastards' they had either been married to or lived with and shit on by. I sat for a while with them, all cackling like old hens, listening to their stories. I knew that those stories must have been repeated, over and over, whenever a new person arrived, like sitting in a nursing home with a room full of Alzheimer patients. It seemed more like a lonely hearts club for the over fifties. Was this what I had to look forward to in my life?

Suddenly the music started, and the first of the ladies from my table jumped to their feet and took to the stage to boogie on down to The Supremes, 'Baby Love', followed by another all-time classic old person's song, Band of Gold together with old Fred who had suddenly become rather animated. It was time for me to leave. I made my excuses and left the building. The exercise had served one purpose and that was to make me smile, for a short time at least.

Mum was getting more and more concerned about me as I started to talk openly about the possibility of suicide. It was an impossible predicament for her to be in: on the one hand, if she told the mental health services how serious this situation was then Faye may have been taken into care; on the other hand if she did nothing and something serious did happen, then Faye wouldn't have a mum anyway. She was caught between a rock and hard place. For days we sat and pondered over the situation and then made a decision; a decision that would almost prove to be fatal.

We talked about me going back to that dreadful place: work. Mum wasn't particularly happy about this but felt powerless to stop me. I thought that maybe the reason I felt so very low was the lack of routine in my life, feeling like a spare part, and not knowing what to do with myself each day. Maybe that was the reason I was falling lower and lower into the vortex of despair and depression.

I talked to the community psychiatric nurse about it whilst trying as hard as I could to look normal, even happy, just to get his consent. I knew I was lying, but I felt I had no choice in the matter. My debts were escalating and no money was coming into the house. No one had informed me that I was entitled to benefits at this point, as they all assumed that I would already know that, given my occupation. Everyone had their roles and they stuck to them like glue and paper. 'I'm a community psychiatric nurse; you'll have to go to the Citizens Advice for that kind of advice.' I hated that attitude and avoiding placing more pressure on people already under strain in my own practice. I wasn't well enough to visit anyone let alone navigate my way through the complexities of the benefit system. It had been six months since I first came out of work and yet I still felt so ill. I knew that if I didn't act now then I would lose the house. I would lose everything I had worked so hard to achieve.

I also knew I would struggle with work – I couldn't even work out how to solve situations like my pen running out of ink – but even though I knew it was a really bad decision, I felt as if I had been pushed into a corner. I had no option but to try and get back into work.

I had to jump through several hoops before getting to sit at my desk again. The first person I had to see was my GP, which wasn't exactly hard as I had recently changed surgeries and the doctors at the new surgery didn't really know me. They didn't seem to really be that bothered about my life so, a quick five-minute appointment and I was signed fit for work. The second person was the psychiatrist, and that was easy too. He also didn't have much interest in me and had never paid a great deal of attention to the state of my mental health in the last two months, so he thought that I was doing great. How wrong could he have been? In his broken English he commented that, 'It would be a good thing for you to go back to your nice job with your nice house and your beautiful daughter and be happy, as you have nothing to be sad about.' So far it was a piece of piss.

Then I had a back-to-work interview with my manager, and that was hard. After all, she did know me and she knew exactly how ill I had been. She wasn't fooled but wanted to give me the benefit of the doubt, so after the occupational health doctor believed me when I said I was well enough, I was declared 'fit for work'.

On my first day back I was immediately panicky. I felt highly embarrassed for having caused a riot in social services earlier in the year and I was enormously paranoid, something that escalated as the weeks passed. I found it hard to communicate with anyone and I didn't fit anywhere, at home or at work.

At home I had no idea how to cope with Faye, whose behaviour was becoming more and more extreme. And at work, despite a phased return, fear was growing inside me.

People were looking at me and whispering amongst themselves, but still trying to act normal around me. I had completely forgotten how to do social work, not understanding what was placed before me. I didn't know what I was doing; I was a fraudster, an imposter. The cases seemed hugely complex and I was frightened to death that I was going to make mistakes. Had I ever known what I was doing? All those decisions that I had made in my life – had they all been wrong? Had people always just tolerated me as an incompetent worker?

I sat at my desk and looked at five different-coloured files sitting in my in tray. I took the top one and started to read. A family member had reported to social services that he thought his niece was being sexually abused by her step-father. He had been in England for the last year and was from Ghana. He had taken the child out of the country for a while and when she

171

returned, she was displaying concerning behaviours. I felt sick to the pit of my stomach and I wanted to run to the toilet.

This was my phased return. This was my shit life. This was a tray full of child abuse cases. But what should I have expected? A case where a child had had his ice cream stolen? This was a serious team, and serious cases were what we dealt with on a daily basis. I had been removed from it for a long time and I knew I wasn't in a mental state to deal with any of it. I asked for a few joint visits to get me back into the swing of things but I sensed no one wanted to be near me. I couldn't do it, I just simply couldn't do it and I knew I was about to be found out.

I had been surveying tower blocks for some weeks. I needed to see which were accessible. The drive up to the door of each one was scary, my heart pounding so hard that I could hear each beat. I tried their doors but couldn't get in, all of them having a minicoms system. There was a deep, driving force within me, a voice that kept egging me to do it. It told me that I was weak and mocked me for not even being able to manage this. I had to find somewhere.

I saw my community psychiatric nurse two days before I went to work on that particular day and told him the full situation. He made an appointment to see me a week later.

On the 8th October 2004 I left for work, knowing that I could no longer continue. I had failed everyone and I was a complete fuck up, a fraud and – most importantly – I was causing my own child pain. I was the one-stop-shop of total disasters. I didn't know how to be any more, I didn't know how to parent, let alone try and make her happy and well. She was struggling at school and being bullied but I didn't know how to stop it. I couldn't stop it.

I got out of the car and walked over to the edge of the car park. I was on the twelfth floor. I felt sick.

I got my briefcase out of the car and looked over the side

of the building once again. On the building opposite, a man was doing some repairs and he was just below my eye level; he glanced over. I walked to the staircase. I had a burning feeling throughout my body.

The voice kept coming into my head.

You chicken shit, you can't even do this, can you? You're so hopeless and useless – no one wants you. Get it over with! The desire to die was stronger than ever.

I walked back to the edge of the car park. I climbed onto the wall, which was about three foot high and I looked down. I moved from a kneeling position to a standing position. I couldn't breathe with anxiety; my hands were shaking, body trembling with fear. I moved back from standing to kneeling and I stepped down from the ledge and returned to my car. I was supposed to be at work by now.

Thinking to myself, *They won't miss me, they're probably glad that I'm not there,* I got a piece of paper and a pen out and started to scribble a note, 'To my darling Faye.' I hadn't thought about leaving a note. How could I have been so selfish for not even leaving a note to tell Faye how much I loved her.

I struggled to hold onto the pen that seemed to jump around in my hand.

'I am so sorry for this, I love you so much my darling child.'

I screwed the paper up. How could I write this note? How could I be so insensitive, insulting almost. I kept thinking how awful this was. I had really struggled as a parent, not really knowing what I had let myself in for when I gave birth. I was naturally maternal but also naturally sociable, so the loneliness of single parenthood had been traumatic. Parenting as a whole had been traumatic but I had done it single-handed and I was soon to be at the finishing point, the point where she had grown and would soon be an adult. I had survived the hardest part, and that's why this made no sense.

I thought about the first time I had held her in my arms and the love I had felt looking at her face, so fragile, so dependent. She was a gift that had been given to me to not only save my life but also to show me I was capable of loving, capable of feeling. Where had that gone? Why would I want to wreck her life now by doing this to her? I knew it would devastate her. I knew she would never get over it if I killed myself. But I couldn't connect with that feeling.

The voice in my head was taking over my thoughts again. I tried once more to write her a letter, to leave her something to explain why I was doing this but there was no explanation for it. Not one that I could comprehend. It felt even weaker than the act itself. She knew why I was doing this; she knew how ill I was. I didn't have a place anymore. I couldn't be at work; I couldn't be at home. I was like a rabbit caught between the headlights of fast moving traffic each side of me. Several times I walked to the edge and back to the car again. Several times I sat in the car in silence, my head in my hands.

There were no tears; I was past tears. Just fear; fear of the unknown. Normal emotions had gone a long time ago. I tried one last time to rid myself of the thought but it would not leave me. I was infected. I was going to die.

For one last time, I climbed onto the ledge and straightened myself up. I knew I couldn't turn back. I took one step forward and off I went, falling, falling, falling, down, down, smash.

THIRTEEN

Reverberation
Sometime in October 2004

Questions I've been asked since jumping off a very tall building:

Did it dent the concrete?
Did you land and squash anyone?
What were you wearing?
Did you have nice shoes on?
Were you scared?
Did you leave a note?
Did it hurt?

'Open thi legs lass and let me wesh ya fanny.' The delightful words of larger than life, no-nonsense, auxiliary nurse standing in my doorway wearing latex rubber gloves and holding a round, yellow bowl of warm water.

I waited eagerly for the punch line.

'Come on lass, ya wain't get a better offer than that, not round here.' And there it was, the punch line. Broken, traumatised, confused and in severe pain, and I was being reminded by 'Mrs Mop A Lot' that if my love life was non-existent before my lemming act, then it sure enough was now.

'You cannot be serious,' I said.

I had been through many things in my life, but this was definitely the most frightening.

'It's all fine, I think I can take it from here, thank you.'

What the hell was going on? What had I been reduced to? It was not meant to be like this. It wasn't that long since I had been running around court in my cotton and polyester mix little black number, black patent heels and thirty denier stockings. Ironed, polished, combed and straightened and now... now within a few short months my life had been changed.

I had changed into something completely unrecognisable. Before, I had had the world in the palm of my hand: I was thirty-four, I had a good career, I had a degree, a child and a home and now it felt as if it was slipping away from me faster than I could stop it. With so many injuries people were shocked that I had survived.

A decision must have been taken at some point to move me to Huntsman Seven, the orthopaedic ward. It was a bit late to consider a mental health ward for me. They, the mental health professionals had said that it was 'no place for people like me'. They didn't want people like me mingling with what they termed 'people like them', referring to other seriously mentally ill people in crisis. Although, I wasn't sure whether they were trying to protect me from them or them from me. Whatever they meant, they had certainly managed to paint a bleak enough picture of the mental health inpatient setting to put off even the hardest and toughest from going there. I was a 'care in the community' person and that 'care' had not been 'good enough' care and this was the result of it. Instead of skipping through wildflower meadows at sunset in my Primark flats and Matalan shawl I now lay here on my supreme, unique electric motion bed wondering whether or not I will ever be able to walk again, whether I will be able to keep my legs, and whether or not I will ever, in my life, be able to return to any kind of work.

Work had always been a central theme to my life, the thing

that defined me (as a person). I needed work for sanity and I was good at my job. I had made mistakes but I was not a failure like some people would be thinking, I was a good social worker and now no one will ever let me work in that capacity again. That made me scared, scared not only where I would fit in society but frightened of how vulnerable Faye and I were in a world where people with disability are viewed as second-class citizens, a benefits system that punishes those who need the support the most. This was the world I was entering into now and I was ill prepared.

As I lay in my bed, I started to feel angry that I had been so let down by services. They had told me they thought I was bipolar a few months earlier, but I didn't really understand what that would mean for me. I hadn't really heard of the term before and although I had attempted to link up with a local self-help group prior to my incident, I hadn't been well enough to engage or participate properly. Jo, one of the senior group members, had taken time out to help me. Jo had also had a career similar to my own and had followed a similar journey into mental ill health. She attempted to take me under her wing and tried hard to involve me back into the land of the living, but it proved an impossible task for I was too far gone for her to save. All I had wanted to do was to not be here, to die.

Trying to make sense of it now was futile. I was the joker, the one that made people laugh but behind the smiles there was darkness and an inability to express the deep depression that had consumed me from a very early age. It was a juxtaposition: on the one hand I had loved life and revelled in my friendships and my love affairs but on the other, each day was an effort. The chronic insomnia, that started when I was just a small child, had really taken a hold in later life and treating it with more anti-depressants had proven fatal. Had the bipolar disorder prevented me from sleeping or did the lack of sleep cause the symptoms of bipolar? I just didn't know.

My nervous energy would cause me to run round the block at four o'clock in the morning, everything felt chaotic: work, home, love, everything. Everything that seemed to make normal people sleep had the opposite effect on me. The hours in the gym, the swimming pool and the running all served to make me more awake and, despite my body suffering total exhaustion, I never stopped. Of course you couldn't see this, no one could. I looked healthy enough. I hid it away, like an affair or a dirty disease. Insomnia was my secret. Alcohol only served to knock me out for a time, three hours max. I'd gotten through twenty-two bottles of Kalms, fourteen bottles of Nitol, seven bottles of Rescue Remedi, five trips to a Homeopath prescribing Acronite, Nux Vomica,Hyoscyamus Niger, Sulphur, Belladonna, Chamomilla, Arsenic Album, and Argenticum Nitricum and still no sleep.

Repeatedly I presented at the doctor's with the same secret, my insomnia. 'Take more of these,' they would say whilst handing me a script for yet more anti-depressants. They sold them well to me. 'Look at it like this,' they would say, 'think of your brain having a test tube in it, when you get stressed, your serotonin gets depleted. This little tablet will make your test tube full again!'

I listened and swallowed, as that's what you do when doctors tell you what's best for you, after all they are the experts. They even wrongly diagnosed and treated my pneumonia with anti-depressants. Prozac, Citralopram, Mirtazapine, Seroxat and Venlafaxine. I was a walking pharmacy. They stopped believing that there could be anything else wrong with me other than depression. No tests or sleep clinic was offered into my chronic insomnia, just more and more pills. I had become the petri dish of biomedicine, the experimental patient, and I had fallen apart.

In my hospital bed, I desperately wanted to comfort my child and explain to family why this had happened but I couldn't. I knew people would want tangible answers, but how could I give answers if I didn't understand this myself? And I didn't understand any of it really. There were so many elements to this, I hardly knew where to begin.

Before I left high dependency, a guy in green overalls came to tell me that my old manager from the Looked After Children Team had rung and wanted to come and see me. Word must have got around quickly about my 'lemming act'. I knew I would be the subject of much gossip. 'Tell him he can come and see me when I've found my feet,' he laughed and I knew John would feel better knowing that I still had a sense of humour. 'Do you think it's possible for you to contact the mental health team and ask my worker to come and see me please?' I asked when he returned to my bed to fiddle with yet more lines going into my neck.

'Of course I can,' he said, 'what's the guy's name?' I told him his name and off he went. He wasn't gone long before returning, 'He wants to know what you want to talk to him about?' I couldn't see his face as I didn't have my contact lenses in or my glasses but in his voice I could sense his feeling of disappointment at the process. 'Isn't it obvious what I want to speak to him about?' infuriated that I was even being asked the question.

My hospital bed was electric, it moved up, down and side-to-side, and for that I was extremely grateful. In the first few days there was little I could do other than press the buttons on the remote control. It was a state-of-the-art bed, super-adjustable with a hi-low motorised frame, a full lock and steer for manoeuvrability at any height, whilst showcasing embedded patient controls and the extendable deck length for the taller patient. I might have been a fucked-up mess, but I was a fucked-up mess in a supreme machine.

Apart from the occasional trip down to X-ray and theatre, each day was much the same. Like clockwork, everything took place in a strict routine just like being back at home living with Mum. Lights on at 7am, cup of tea at 7.30am, wash at 8am, breakfast at 8.30am, doctors' visits at 9am and so on. The routine of it all had a certain comforting feeling to it. It was a comfort just to be alive so the ordinariness was welcomed with open arms. Mum had had strict routines, even down to the rota of mealtimes: liver and sausages on a Monday, flan and chips on a Tuesday, fish supper on a Friday and a cooked breakfast on a Sunday. It had crossed my mind whether my rebelling to the routine of this monotonous existence had indeed been the single cause of my demise. Whatever routines were imposed upon me, sleep still didn't come.

I laid flat on my back with the head-rest up; I hadn't moved from that position since they brought me out of the induced coma. I couldn't move. I was stuck and I didn't know whether this was a permanent 'stuck' or a temporary stuck. A small part of me was glad of the opportunity to have a reason not to move, to be this 'stuck'. I needed to be stuck to heal.

I deliberated on whether this was the place that I had always meant to have been. As if God – if there is a God – had broken every bone in my body just to get me to stop and take stock of my life, to stop me from running faster and faster like a speed train without the brakes. Maybe this had been his way of keeping me safe in a bizarre, macabre way.

But I didn't believe in God, because if there was a God that could affect things like this then why did he allow bad things to happen to children in distress? Why did he not stop the parent from throwing the baby at the window? If he had affected my 'gentle lowering to the ground' as it had been suggested by one of the Jesus Army helpers, then why did he allow such heinous crimes against vulnerable children to occur?

Just thinking about child protection made me feel unwell. Just as I was getting used to lying in one place, not daring to move, as each movement was more excruciating than the last, a doctor appeared and give the go ahead for me to be hoisted onto a chair. Now I was really scared.

Hoisting required careful consideration, precision and navigation. The entire operation took no fewer than six staff just to move me under two feet. Pushing me onto my spine, they tried to slide the material under me and hook me up to an A-frame machine. Like Free Willy being moved from the aquarium to the deep ocean I was lifted, spun, twisted and released into my final resting spot, the Shackletons chair next to the bed. A real achievement for everyone involved. In fact, in the beginning, it was such an achievement that everyone cheered as I slumped in my plastic-covered Layburn, only to slide, moments later, onto the floor as the blood rushed to the head causing me to faint.

Twenty minutes a day I withstood the humiliation of being hauled from bed to chair and the torture of trying to sit up straight and not slide onto the floor. This would go on until someone came to my aide, which could take anything from twenty minutes to an hour, depending on how busy the ward was. Sit, watch, wait, pass out, back in hoist, back to bed. My life in four weeks, my sole achievements for that period of time: wash my own private parts, change my own colostomy and hold on for dear life for twenty minutes' sitting time. They soon got bored with the complicated mechanics of it all and left me in peace with my Celebrations, nicotine gum and a copy of Paul McKenna *Change Your Life in Seven Days* book, for a short time anyway.

I fitted in well with the grey walls in the room I was placed in. It was small and compact, with a sink to my right and a small window with old, faded curtains that led out to the corridor on E bay, the ward my room was situated on. I had my own room as I was testing positive for MRSA: I had the 'My Red Shiny Arse' disease, the killer infection. I longed for the sink to get up and move a few feet nearer to my bed so I could turn the tap on and rinse my face and feel the cool water on my hands and my fingers.

The stoma bag was my biggest concern. I had been told that I had it on because my spine had perforated my bowel and they had done it to save my life. They said it was likely to be permanent. I didn't want to touch it to look at it. I didn't want to ever eat again in the hope that I would never have to change it. It had been placed right in the middle of my stomach. Usually they are placed on a person's hips but they also explained to me that both my hips had exploded out of my body so it was the only position they could possibly put it. I hated possessions at the best of times. I hated things girls are supposed to like, like jewellery and, most of all, I hated bags. Now I had my very own bag that was permanently stuck to the front of my stomach: my new 'shit bag'. I tried to comfort myself with a Mars Bar Celebration and look on the bright side – at least I wouldn't have to get up to go to the loo and miss *Coronation Street*. It did little to appease my anguish.

I wanted desperately to talk to someone about why this had happened. I needed an explanation for how I had come to be so unwell.

Being on Huntsman was a relief. It was like being laid on a bed in the middle of a busy railway station. Every team in the hospital must have visited me, even plastics. After falling over eighty-five feet I had absolutely no visible injuries on any part of my body apart from a tiny inch-long cut sitting neatly under my lower lip, a consequence of biting into the bottom half of my face as I hit the concrete.

Everyone wanted questions answering, questions, questions and more questions. When I spoke they all scribbled, when the surgeons spoke they all scribbled. Then they left. Then the best people started to arrive. I woke early one day to find four very handsome and smart men standing around my bedside, all cupping their chins, pondering; under different circumstances this would have most definitely have been the most fun day of my life, sadly it was not a sex game and this was not a fun situation.

Mr Blundell, Mr Royston, Mr Davis and another orthopaedic surgeon were all chattering amongst themselves about my feet. My 'experimental feet'. These guys were the 'foot men'. The men that were going to try out a new pioneering experiment to help me save my feet and pave the way for future surgery.

They had already met me but I had never met them. This was the first time they had ever seen anything like this, and there was no precedent for mending something quite so 'messy' as they put it. Rubbing their chins in synchronicity they began to draw up a plan as to what to do next with the flesh and bone that was being held together with plaster casts and all they needed to do was to sell their idea to me.

The situation felt so unreal. I was overwhelmed by a sense of loss, guilt and despair that I had failed as a mother, as a daughter and as a professional. Mother made it quite clear that she was most unhappy with me. No longer was I Kathryn, the tall blonde one that makes people laugh, the person who all the 'looked-after' kids wanted as their social worker. I had now become 'that woman who threw herself off a building'. The service user, the nutter, the jumper – this was how people would identify me for the rest of my life. I started to cry as they were leaving the room. Mr Davies, who was newly qualified, held back, cupping my hand in his, not knowing what to say when I asked him why this had happened to me.

I wanted to escape far away, to take Faye and start a new life and be someone new. I thought about buying a camper van and travelling the world, or selling my house and moving to a different part of the country with a new identity, but I couldn't get out of bed or turn over so that wasn't going to happen anytime soon.

I worried about returning to my community and how I would be received. Would people know about it? Would they hate me for it or would they understand? It was never going to attract the same empathy and well wishes that having an illness like cancer or being in a car crash would have. People would be suspicious, embarrassed and afraid. Most of all I worried about Faye.

It was going to be hard. I knew there would be people who I had cared about who would shun me, people who may have had their own experiences of suicide who would bring their baggage to my situation, or people who just thought I had done this heinous act because I was selfish or attention seeking. I knew that wasn't the case and so did those who loved me. This had happened because I cared too much, tried too hard and could not cope. I tried to put the worry to the back of my mind and concentrate on what lay ahead in my immediate future, like how I could survive another operation. I couldn't visualise how life outside of here would function, and whether there would be a future at all for Faye and me.

A week went by and many people passed through my room bringing love, grapes, flowers and forced humour. It was unbearable, too hard to face people. Many tears were shed out of relief that I had survived, but also out of bewilderment and fear. Friends had been waiting to visit for weeks but couldn't, as my family had placed restrictions on people coming to intensive care: they didn't want people to see me like that, swollen and unconscious. Sadly, some people didn't adhere to this request and barged their way in. I had no idea of this at the time and, strangely, none of those people came when I was conscious. It left me with a weird feeling, like I'd been observed by almost strangers, at my lowest point.

I'd been on Huntsman ward for about a week. A guy in a wheelchair passed by my room and peered in. I shouted for him to come in and we got chatting. His name was Martin.

Martin had had the whole of his right leg and his hip removed due to botulism, a disease that you can get from the soil. This made no sense to me at first but as we got to know each other over the weeks, Martin began to tell me his history.

He knew the inner workings of the hospital system better than the people who worked there: he had been an inpatient for seven months and had been kicked out of the room I was in to be put on the ward. For a while he was annoyed with me about that, but he soon got over it. Martin had originally been placed in my room to die. No one thought he would survive what he had been through. He had even been allowed to smoke in there prior to me moving in, which explained why it smelt like a pub tap room. They had made many allowances for Martin based on the fact that the odds of him surviving were minimal.

He loved being in hospital. He knew how it worked and he functioned well there; he was institutionalised. Best of all, he knew how to get the best food.

He called me 'Kat', which I hated but never stopped him because he liked to wind me up. 'Don't bother with that hospital shite' – referring to the food – 'order Halal,' he said, with the cheekiest grin you had ever seen.

'You'll have the best curries in town, they're made in Bradford and sent down, and you can get naan bread and pilau rice.' Martin was a minefield of information.

'If they ask you any questions, tell 'em you're a Muslim and that you converted before you jumped. They can't prove you're not, they don't do blood tests for it you know.'

His Del Boy style, a cute combination of innocence, mischievousness and anti-authoritarian approach to life made me laugh. I came to love the way he was and it carried me through the darkest days and nights in the months following the incident.

We became close friends and spent days and nights together

talking, sharing stories, crying, laughing and playing games, drinking beer and wine that my friends had bought for us to share. I did all the crying, he did all the cheering up.

Martin had a way about him that made everyone love him almost immediately. Perhaps it had been his way of surviving for so long; perhaps he was happy that finally he was living a less chaotic life.

We were two people from completely different backgrounds, meeting in this most unusual circumstance with one massive thing in common: we had been stopped and we had been saved.

As we got closer, Martin revealed information about his past to me: he said that he had grown up in care. He, along with his five siblings, had been abandoned on the doorstep of an orphanage in Nottingham by his mother who had met a new man and opted for a new life in Japan. Just like that, five children etched away from her life, deserted. He described the orphanage as being a hundred-bed unit, which I found hard to imagine. He was two years old when he was left there and his mother had never returned to England for them since that day.

His happiest memories were living in the orphanage, as his subsequent foster homes left a lot to be desired. He had had fourteen foster placement breakdowns in eight years. Some he had suffered horrific abuse in but he was careful not to share this with me, given the state I was in. At the age of fifteen he had run away and begun his career, his lifetime addiction to heroin, the white powder that would eventually lead him to the point of near death and to me. He had injected in his femoral vein and this had proved to be lethal.

He had detoxed whilst in a coma for three months, which had given him a massive head start on the road to recovery, but he was still on a methadone programme. Martin found it humorous, that for most of his childhood, he had had social workers. Some had been good, some were bad, and now he had become friends with one who was occupying his old bed, in the room that they had placed him in to die some nine months earlier. He felt a great sense of pride that he was able to help me, rather than being on the receiving end of support for once in his life. We had a truly phenomenal exchange.

He had a strong sense of altruism and moral code of what was right and wrong. He hated injustice and he hated suffering. He made sure the elderly patients got what they needed, often helping to feed them or get them things from the shop. He knew their names, and they adored him like he adored them. Within that setting he was trusted, and that was something he had never experienced. I trusted him.

Martin had limited visitors so he took to sharing mine. My friends would bring him beer and cigarettes in and he was always welcome at visiting time.

Due to the severity of my injuries, I was prevented from having a wheelchair. Dr Martin had other plans for me. He wanted me out of bed and outside to see the world, even if it did mean him putting me at risk. My back was broken in several places, my pelvis had exploded out of my body, my femur was broken, my hands, my sternum and my clavicle bone smashed to bits, but the thing that had taken the most impact was my feet. Both feet were completely smashed, splattered like pancakes. They had put them both in plaster casts and, at the time, I had thought they would just stay on for a few months and be removed in due course, and then everything would be fine.

Martin set about planning on building me a wheelchair out of bits and pieces of broken chairs laying around the hospital and, using a small toolkit he had cadged off a visitor, he and his accomplice – Mark, another amputee – began assembling my new chair.

After a few days, the orthopaedic consultants returned to

my bedside. Mr Blundell took the lead in explaining that, after careful consideration, they had four options to get me walking again. He explained that thousands of little bones were floating around in my feet and it would be impossible to ever fully repair them.

In much less technical terms, he explained that option one was to leave my feet to heal on their own with no invasive surgery, a kind of 'suck it and see' approach to see if the bones would fuse themselves together in time.

Option two was to chop off both my legs below the knee and have prosthetic limbs.

Option three was that they could attempt to pin and plate some of the larger bones together which would be difficult, to say the least.

Or option four was something new, an unprecedented idea of putting me in some boots.

Now, when Mr Blundell said 'boots', what he didn't say was what these boots would look like. In fact, he didn't exactly elaborate that much at all. Rather like trying to get a child to choose something you yourself want them to choose, by emphasising the positive option in favour of the others, he made it sound like the best option. I imagined leather boots, preferably black, that came to my knee, maybe with some metal down the side. I thought they could look quite rock and roll. However, that was not what I got.

I was wheeled down to theatre and, after a six-hour operation, I emerged and, to my horror, I had two round, three-tier metal mechanic sets peering out from beneath the covers. My Izalof frames.

Nothing like the sexy leather boots I had visualised.

The pain was indescribable, and they looked like a prop from a horror movie. Martin entered my room and burst out laughing.

'What the fuck!' he exclaimed. 'What the fuck do you look

like?' he could not stop laughing and even though I was crying he continued to laugh.

Rings of metal were held with rods that had been inserted through my skin and into my bones, like an oversized, scary acupuncture kit, and they were stuck on the end of my feet. My feet looked alien. Wrapped in red swaddling, my feet were suspended in these frames of horror: my 'experimental feet. The ground-breaking, pioneering treatment of these seriously mashed-up body parts was complete. The threaded rods on each side went up my leg and ended five inches below my knee.

I was the unique specimen demonstrating how non-invasive surgery could be used to stimulate bone growth for faster healing and better outcomes. For a time, I was the star of the show, the leading lady of the foot and ankle department. Pictures of my 'experimental feet' adorned the walls of the outpatient department and surgical papers were written on me. Was this the fame I had been searching for, my recognition? For a time I had the most interesting feet of the entire hospital.

*

Day after day, night after night, I lay in the grey room, staring at the ceiling, the walls and at the roof. I could see through the window. I dreamed of being at home with Faye. Loving her, laughing with her, looking after her like a proper mother. The times that I did sleep I would wake in a panic, with the realisation that this was now my reality.

I dreamed of getting out of bed and walking to the sink, cupping the fresh, cool water in my hands and splashing my face. The frames on my feet got tangled every few hours and I had to ask for help to unlock myself. They ripped through each pair of sheets that were put on until I came up with a brilliant idea: external fixator foot warmers – that's what I needed. The next time Mum visited I asked her to get some fluffy fabric and make me a pair of oversized bags with drawstrings around the tops.

'Would it be possible to be hoisted to the bathroom so I can have a bath?' I asked one of the nurses. She looked at me, knowing that this was going to be a mammoth task involving several people and a lot of hard work.

'I am really sorry, but I feel so unbearably dirty.'

I had had my period and, although they tried hard to help me wash, nothing could replace the deep clean that you get from a bath. My body was screaming to be in water.

I dreaded being lifted, the pain was hard but the embarrassment was even more unbearable. One of the support staff had been given the task to help. She rolled me over and laid half the sling beneath my right side, then rolled me the other way to pull it through. The first part of the hoisting was the worst, the lift off. Once in the air I could relax. I needed one member of staff per foot, to hold my frames and move them around the corners in line with the machine. The bathroom was only two doors up and, as I was wheeled in all my glory down the corridor, passers-by gawped at the spectacle.

Once in the bathroom I breathed a sigh of relief. Sarah had run the bath but there was a problem: she couldn't get the cold tap to work. I clung on for dear life, dangling over the burning hot bath, like a stamp being steamed from an envelope and a tea bag waiting to be plunged into the cup.

'I'm just going to pop out and see if I can get help,' she announced. Momentarily I trusted her.

Sarah was a small, plump-looking woman in her mid-thirties. She had a habit of zoning out whilst staring, fixated, at your face. It was both unnerving and slightly irritating but, given the predicament I was in, it was no time to be criticising the staff's personality traits. She was there and she was prepared to bathe me, and that was all that mattered to me. I didn't care if she had green hair and spoke Tuyuca, all I cared about was the clean, warm water.

She left the room. In front of me was a large, horizontal, rectangular-shaped mirror. For the first time I could see myself: stark naked with metal on my feet, hanging in a cloth over a bath.

I hated myself. I hated what I had done to myself, the grief I had caused and the subsequent consequences of my actions. I thought about the money that I had selfishly used from the NHS that could have been used to save the lives of those that deserved to live, and I wanted this to stop but it wasn't going to, not ever.

I didn't know if this situation was permanent or whether I may recover. And if I did recover, nobody knew to what extent that would be. They had no precedent so it was hard for them to determine what would happen next, what my recovery would look like.

Fifteen minutes of purgatory must have passed by and still no Sarah. There were limited staff on that day and I knew that the bathroom was far away from the main desk. I waited patiently, which was something I wasn't good at. More time passed and it became clear that Sarah was not coming back. I panicked, but knew that someone was bound to see I was missing from my bed. Or would they? People might think I had gone for an X-ray: I had spent most of my early days in X-ray so it wouldn't be unusual, although they usually took me on my bed and the bed was still there.

'Help!' I shouted, in the hope that someone would hear my plea.

'Help, I'm stuck!'

No one came.

The door was a thick fire door and I didn't know how sound proof the room was. I could see the emergency cord but I couldn't reach it. More time passed, and I knew the bath must have cooled down, so she had clearly forgotten me. I started to swing in a vain attempt to reach the cord. Like *Indiana Jones and the Temple of Doom*, I risked life and limb to reach the cord. The swings started slowly, gently rocking. As they got bigger, the lift started to shake. I wasn't far away now, a little higher and I will have reached it, I was close, so close. The feet of the hoist were lifting off the floor with each swing. 'Yes!' I shouted at the top of my voice as I grabbed the cord, pulling it hard. The nurses came running. Help had finally arrived.

★

After a couple of weeks of having the fixators on, the physiotherapists told me that they wanted me up and walking. This didn't seem like a possibility. How could I walk with these frames on my feet? The fixators came down lower than my feet, for a start, and they had a rod of steel that went through the ball of my ankle so I would be walking on that. I would be walking on the frame whilst my feet pushed down to the floor, dragging the metal through my skin. The occupational therapists made some bizarre-looking strap-on sandal-type shoes that helped to cushion the feet. Held together with Velcro, the hideous inventions served their purpose for I was nearly ready to fully weight bear by being lifted into an upright position. Out came the stand-up hoist.

It wasn't just me that had to be manoeuvred, but all the wiring that was attached to me too. It all had to be carefully reorganised and dismantled. Tubes fed in on both sides and I had a catheter, three drips and a nebuliser that all had to be removed, reinserted and reattached. The whole operation was a logistical nightmare. For a couple of weeks I was lifted into a standing position, each time being expected to weight bear more and more. At first I fainted every time. Eventually, when this had stopped, they took the hoist away and I was left standing alone. Nurses came into the room to witness the event. I was upright without assistance and this was a miracle.

Over the course of a few months I made great progress with walking. Martin would watch on, sometimes laughing, sometimes encouraging, usually both. He could see I was getting better and better. He had started his rehabilitation too and was enjoying going to the gym over the road once a day. He was learning to walk with a full prosthetic leg that had an unsightly strap round it as he had no hip. We were both on the right path.

They still wouldn't give me a wheelchair though and I now wanted to go outside to feel the fresh air on my skin. Martin and Mark were well on the way to having my new superb, recycled wheelchair ready for me and I was ready for it.

The worst thing about being in hospital was nothing to do with the staff or the pain, it was not being able to be there for Faye. I knew I had caused her so much upset, fear and confusion, and things at home were not good.

Mum had moved into my house and she just couldn't cope with the situation. It cut to my very core. A friend, Fiona, did her best to help by having Faye overnight once a week which helped Faye a lot but it wasn't right that I was in here and she was out there. I asked if she could move in with me but they wouldn't allow that. Each time she came, I reached out to her soul and pleaded with her to hang on for us, to show bravery and be a strong girl. I told her that she needed to be stronger than she had ever had to be before. The pain burned inside me, and this pain couldn't be relieved with morphine.

I had to feel it. This was the cross that I had to bear.

We often wept together. It was as if the trauma of this event had woken me up. The pain, both physical and emotional, forced me to have feelings again, and these strong feelings were bringing me back to life. I had woken up from the deep pit of despair, only to find myself in a much deeper pit, a much blacker and far more frightening place, a place where all my control and independence had been removed. I could not run or hide from this and I had to face it. I had to face each day, and each new challenge that presented itself to me.

I worried about work and I worried about our lives but I knew that there was nothing I could do to change anything. I had put myself in a place where it seemed I needed to be at that time. A place where I was forced to look at myself, my life and my future.

Faye came most days and lovingly helped with my personal care. She showed such strength and courage that it was hard to believe she was only fourteen. I worried for her constantly, for she was left in the outside world, a world that was chaotic and unpredictable. Social services were no help at all. One social worker who had met with her had arranged to meet her in town. Faye went but the worker had failed to turn up. No phone calls, no nothing. The same social worker had also arranged to come and meet me but had, again, failed to turn up. The counselling she was receiving at school sounded more like lecturing. It was a hard situation all round.

The mental health team eventually came to see me. They came in their masses to protect themselves, no doubt, from any comments that were made that might lead to a complaint. I didn't want their help. They had been of no use to me before and they were of no use to me now. They conducted a bizarre assessment to see if I was still feeling suicidal which was a joke, as even if I was there was little I could have done about it in here. I couldn't even get out of bed alone. They paid lip service to offering me the usual counselling services but there was nothing really tangible. I needed help with Faye at home:

that was my only concern, and it seemed that no one could offer me that.

It had been a long time since I had spoken to Barry and I wondered if he had heard what had happened to me. He had been on my mind a lot and I looked at the phone above my bed. I hoped that it would ring, and that one day I would answer it and it would be him.

'Hello, Barry here, how are you?'

I longed to hear his voice, but in a more rational way than before. I had bigger things concerning me now, like walking independently and parenting my child. He didn't ring, and I knew he couldn't, he probably didn't even know about it. With each passing week my mental health improved. One day I lay looking at the phone wondering whether, if I did phone Barry, he would be allowed to speak to me. Curiosity got the better of me so I lifted the receiver and dialled the number, the same number that was etched in my memory. The male receptionist answered.

'I would like to speak to Barry White, please.'

My tone was calm and polite, unrecognisable from the months of shouting obscenities down the phone.

'Err, err,' he hesitated, and then asked, 'who is calling please?'

'Kathryn. Kathryn Littlewood,' I declared.

'Just putting you through, Kathryn,' he said.

I couldn't believe it; it was that easy! I didn't even have to make up a silly name or disguise my voice, not that any of that had ever worked. Had he really just said he was putting me through?

They had been so clear that Barry was not to speak to me again and I never, ever thought that they would back down on that. My heart started to beat really fast: in one second, Barry was going to speak. In one second, I would hear his lovely soft, intoxicating voice again.

'Hello you,' he said.

It was him; his voice softer than normal, if that was at all possible. I could hear concern in his voice but he remained steadfastly professional. 'Hello you,' he said again when I failed to respond to him the first time out of shock and disbelief.

'Oh Barry,' I exhaled a sigh of relief; 'it's really you!'

'Yes. I haven't got long as they don't know I have taken this call from you so I only have a few minutes, OK?'

He had always liked to make sure I fully understood the situation and the amount of time he had. He would prepare me for the eventual parting.

'Do you know what I have done?' I asked him nervously.

'Yes I do.' There was an eerie silence between us. I felt a pain in my chest and a tear ran down my face. 'You were very ill, and I am deeply sad about this,' he added, 'deeply saddened.'

He continued, 'Is there a wall near you? Can you reach out and touch it?'

'Yes, there is, there is one behind me and I can just about reach it.'

'Put your hand on the wall and think about your favourite film, do this at 10pm each night.'

I knew exactly what he meant by this statement. Barry was trying to reach out to me by using a code. He knew my all-time favourite film, *Disco Pigs,* and he wanted us to re-enact a sequence in the play. It was about two small children who lived next door to each other, both in difficult circumstances, who would seek comfort from each other by holding hands through a hole in the wall that they had chiselled out. Each night, at the same time, they would fall asleep holding hands.

They had been born on the same day at the same time, and they had a special connection. It was a deep bond that only they understood, but their love for each other proved to have devastating consequences. Like the two children, frightened and afraid, he wanted to comfort me in the only way he could.

Barry loved me, he really did. I did not know when I would speak with him again, or indeed if I ever would, but it didn't matter now. I knew he loved me and I knew that life would play out the way it was going to, regardless of how I tried to change it. He had given me strength and hope and that was what I needed right then, right there.

★

Over the weeks and months I could see Faye's mental health deteriorating. I knew it was time for me to leave the hospital. I still had the fixators on my feet and I was barely walking, but I knew that I had to go home. If I could just get upstairs into bed I was sure the rest of it would fall into place. I didn't know how any of this was going to look and I didn't care; there was no way I was leaving Faye alone at Christmas.

Against the doctors' advice, I discharged myself. They understood why I had to go and they respected my decision to be autonomous in this situation, although they were never entirely happy with it. I had no idea how long the Meccano sets had to stay on my feet but I was determined to get up those stairs with them on. The pin sites were infected badly and were causing tremendous pain, but this paled into insignificance when I thought about Faye's emotional anguish.

I struggled on, trying harder and harder to walk and, within two weeks, I was able to walk down the corridor and back, and I could just about get up the stairs. It was enough to satisfy the doctors that I would be safe.

After only three months, the discharge day eventually arrived and I said my farewells to both the staff and to Martin, who I was the most sad to leave. I vowed to keep in touch. I had made some good friends, friends that I would never have met if this hadn't happened to me. I was sad to leave Martin and worried how I would cope without his support, but I left in the knowledge that we would always have a close bond.

FOURTEEN

Dear Pig
Christmas 2004

COMING HOME WAS DIFFICULT. It wasn't as if I had been away on holiday and was returning to the same place exhausted, toes with sand rubbing between them, tanned, tired and suitcase full of dirty washing. I had returned from something very harrowing and disturbing into the very place where the trauma had begun. This house, my once-lovely home, now held bad memories. I didn't want to be here, but I had no option. Not knowing what to expect or how I would cope, I sat in my wheelchair and gave the key to Faye to open the door. With no adult support at home and no care in place, I wondered how this was going to look. I took a deep breath and pushed myself out of the wheelchair and with both hands I grabbed the doorframe, steadying myself before the next painful move of getting myself with frames on both feet up the step and through the door. Faye had positioned herself inside the house and facing me and holding both her arms out, I grabbed her and put one foot inside leaving the other leg precariously balancing on the step. With the other foot now inside the house I stood surveying the room that I had left that morning, the morning of the 8th October 2004, with the knowledge I would never return. Now face-to-face with Faye, for the first time in four months, standing upright, I was able to hold her properly, tears running down both our cheeks, we knew we had got past the first goal post, we were together again.

Step by step, slowing pushing then pulling me, and with a great deal of assistance from Faye, I managed to get myself to the top of the stairs. I knew it was a dangerous position to be out of hospital without a high level of support and I also knew that Faye had a utopian vision of what this was going to look like. I on the other hand had a very realistic idea of how bad this was going to be and how impossible it was going to be to care not only for myself but for her. She was nearly fifteen and despite her having to grow up very fast over the last few months, she was not familiar with caring for someone to this degree and she was at an age where she needed her mum the most. School had been horrendous for her. They had shoved her in the learning base out of the way; the message I got from them was that it was too distressing for the other kids. School had a lot to answer for but right now, in this moment, there was little I could do to help her. I would be relying on her for support, her and the home delivery guy from Tesco and was hoping and praying that whoever delivered my shopping would be kind enough to bring it in and put the frozen food in the freezer for us and if he was really nice, he might even pack it away in the cupboard and cook us a meal. I slumped backward on my bed. Faye lifted my frames off the floor and placed them, carefully down. She took the warm, fluffy, pink fake fur pullover frame covers Mum had made me and put them on over the frames. The covers had several purposes: one, they kept the metal that penetrated my ankle bones warm; two, they kept my feet warm; three, they stopped the sheets from ripping; four, they stopped the frames from getting stuck together rendering me completely helpless until someone came along to untangle me and lastly, they provided a conversational piece for a dialogue between Mum and I, who just found it too difficult a subject to discuss with me.

'Can we order pizzas?' Faye asked, smiling and crying at the same time as she lay down on the bed next to me, hugging me. 'I knew you would come home Mum,' she said. I wanted to say, 'I was always going to come home darling,' but I couldn't because I knew that just was not true. I didn't expect to have survived this and now I had I didn't know what to expect next. I pulled her as close to me as I could and tucked her head under my chin so I could smell her hair. I loved smelling her hair when she was small and I loved her now just like I loved her when she was a baby. She never had a dad and that made me all the more protective of her. How could I have done this to her? How could I have wanted to leave someone who is more precious to me than my own life? None of it made sense.

'Of course we can, love, you can have anything you want darling,' I replied also knowing that was a lie, a pizza was about the limit of things at the moment. I was facing a life of unemployment now. My career and reputation in tatters and I had spent money that I had borrowed on my mortgage which I could not repay. No one was ever going to employ me now. 'Ham and pineapple love?' her favourite.

Christmas time was looming. The tree stayed in its tattered old cardboard box, held together with frayed bits of string dating back three decades. We didn't feel like trimming up. My feet burned like red-hot pokers had been drilled through them. Self-caring was hard as I could barely make it to the bathroom, let alone be a functioning parent.

*

A week had passed since the external fixators had been removed from my feet and they had been replaced by knee-high black pots that covered my lower limbs. It was a mixed blessing, because although the removal of metal bars that penetrated through both ankle bones and legs brought relief, a bigger problem loomed and I hoped and prayed that this additional, new, excruciatingly painful feeling in my right foot was one which could be fixed.

Despite only being weeks into this journey, I didn't want to have come this far and now start facing the prospect of an amputation. I liked my leg and I wanted to keep it. I had smashed both feet and ankles to pieces and they were bound to be painful but I knew this chronic, relentless pain in my right ankle was not normal and feared it would be with me forever. The nurse came and cut a hole in the plaster cast and it felt like a minor relief. A raging infection was growing inside the bone and the pressure was building inside the plaster cast. With nowhere for the swelling to go, my upper thigh began turning a very bright, colourful purple; back to hospital for yet another stretch.

Christmas was the least of my concerns but, for Faye, I had to try and at least make an effort. Christmases had always been hard, having been a single mum since the age of nineteen. I envied those families who shared, laughed and were happy together.

Our Christmases were consistent: they were predictably painful, dull and lonely times to get through. We were not the reincarnation of the Cadburys Biscuit Tin family nor were we the Walton family, but we had each other, an over-priced turkey crown, some pre-packed frozen sprouts, a tin of carrots and another viewing of *The Sound of Music* and *Shrek*.

Faye's initial excitement at having me home was slowly turning to boredom and anger. She had longed for me to be back at home after the worst three months of her life. She had cleaned, polished and done her very best to prepare the house for my homecoming, she had even thought about getting a few decorations from the loft, but nothing could have prepared her for the journey ahead. Nothing could have prepared either of us for the deep, fluctuating feelings and emotions that she would experience now that I was back. No one can ever feel another person's pain and no one can ever measure their pain threshold against someone else's and it was clear that Faye didn't really understand quite how sick I was. Although mentally I seemed to be doing alright – hitting the concrete with such force had in some way erased the depression – but physically I was a mess. She thought I was going to spring into action, resume my position of being the mother that she knew and loved before I got sick. She had anticipated me laughing, playing with her and generally taking up the role of parenting again. Instead, I was bedridden and severely disabled. I tried to ask her for very little and tried my hardest to get down the stairs to make sure she had food. I gave her my cash card to get food for herself from the shops and any bits and pieces that we needed. I ordered groceries online and had food delivered.

As the days went on, things changed. The feelings of excitement were replaced by intense anger which seemed to grow inside her like a tumour, day by day infecting her soul and changing her personality, her mood and ultimately our relationship.

Being at home and alive just wasn't enough. She wanted something from me yet couldn't express what that something was. She had constructed an impenetrable glass wall around herself, trapping herself alone on the inside and leaving me firmly outside in the remoteness of despair. Her fragility was masked by a tough, masculine, hard character much like the one she adopted during the years of bullying in secondary school in the lead up my illness. Harder and more vicious than before, trapped in a world of despair and anger, she had shut herself off completely. I wanted to climb inside her world and soothe her pain but the pain she felt was down to me and I was the one person she didn't want to be around. She needed someone to talk to outside the home but there was no one there. Family couldn't communicate on this level and had given all they felt able to give. We weren't that close and they had their own lives.

Mistakenly, I was waiting for the mental health team to make a referral for a family therapist or some sort of talking therapy that could help us both to make sense of what had happened, but that was not the case.

No matter how dysfunctional this was, I needed to make Christmas a good day, no matter how shit we felt, and no matter what others thought.

We had opened our presents the night before. My wish had been for Faye to come through this and to find some level of forgiveness and compassion for the events that had happened this year. I prayed that I would soon be able to have a bath. Each movement felt traumatic. Turning, sitting, laughing, crying, everything I'd always taken for granted, the simplest of movements, hurt. This was my cross to bear: I had caused it and I was paying the price.

Early that morning, I went through the usual ordeal of getting to the bathroom and steadying myself with the sink. Not quite sitting, not quite standing and just managing to wash my hair.

I hadn't been near a computer since before the incident. I crawled on my hands and knees into Faye's bedroom. I turned the computer on. The Packard Bell was on its last legs and had suffered its own degree of trauma from me hammering nonsense into the keyboard since I was first ill in March. The sticky, dirty keys from coffee and brandy spills with strands of tobacco and ash stuck between them barely worked and it took an age to load. I dreaded seeing the emails from my mad tirade, a direct reminder of how mental things had been. I signed into Hotmail, my one and only email address.

I leaned back in my office chair as I watched several boxes

appear in the left hand corner of the screen, messages from MSN Chat. Some of them were Faye's friends but one of them caught my eye. It had been sent only moments earlier, and my heart skipped a beat. It read: 'Discopigs@h[...]m wants to add you to messenger.'

I knew immediately who this was.

'It's him! It's bloody well him! He's bloody come to me, just like I always knew he would!' I shouted, but there was only silence as I was home alone. Faye had opted to spend Christmas morning at her friend's house as there was little on offer for her here.

I could hardly contain my excitement. 'Good God it's him, it's really him, its Barry!' I knew he loved me. Deep down inside I always knew he loved me and this now proved my theory, why else would he risk contacting me outside work if he didn't love me?

In my head, I danced joyfully around the room: spinning, arms spread out, jubilant, elated. In reality, I sat back and smiled, smugly and self-contented.

Like a child winning the egg and spoon race for the first time I was overjoyed, this was my Christmas present. Doubt soon followed the excitement though. I began to catastrophise, to look for negatives in the situation. I feared that this was in fact just another illusion, another mind trick like before. This felt different – more real, and definitely more sensible. I was functioning better than before; I was more stable and together. I knew this was neither a figment of my imagination nor an optical illusion. The box with the message was definitely on my screen and it was unquestionably real.

Without a second thought, I clicked 'Add', and waited nervously for a response. I waited and I waited. My fixed spine was sore – without a coccyx bone sitting was hard. An hour went by and nothing. I switched the computer off and crawled back to my bedroom, disappointed.

Only 'he' knew that *Disco Pigs* was my favourite film. Only 'he' could have sent that message. Only weeks ago when I laid on my hospital bed and phoned him from my bedside, he had risked a disciplinary by allowing me to speak with him and it was in that moment he let me know he had listened to me and knew what my favourite film was. He knew my email address and he knew that, at some point, I was coming out of hospital. He also knew he was walking on dangerous ground.

So many questions raced through my mind: if it was him what would I say to him? Would I tell him about all the things I have been doing? Would I show him all the poetry I wrote for him, believing it was him I was writing to? What does he want me for? Does he want to tell me he is married and he never loved me? Had I caused him harm? What if it is a cruel joke? What if he is playing me? Would I tell him how much I am in love with him?

Christmas passed, business as usual. This consisted of turkey, cheese, biscuits, an episode of the *Royle Family* and several glasses of Merlot. I had a spring in my pots that lasted all day and it was nothing to do with the festivities around me, as they were fairly absent. We were transported off to an uncomfortable family dinner where I had the 'you have jumped off a very tall building and we don't know what to say about it' seat at the head of the table and predictably, no one spoke a word about the 'incident'. Everyone was silent, all apart for my stoma bag that kept letting out undesirable noises that I had no control over, prompting giggles from around the table. I couldn't wait to get home and, unsurprisingly, no one was begging us to stay. It was an uncomfortable situation for everyone, and I had more important things to do in any case, like checking my email again.

As soon as I got in I logged onto the computer. Faye immediately disappeared off to her mate's house to compare how much money they had managed to procure out of relatives and check out each other's new mobile phones – the distance and disconnect between us growing bigger with each passing day.

Fixated on what was to be the next installment of this story, I sat back and watched the screen as it loaded, making whirring noises similar to a washing machine. I patiently sat fingers crossed while the computer loaded and there it was, right there where I had hoped and prayed it would be, my email, my long awaited, personal, away from his work, email. The private lines of communication with Mr Barry White were now well and truly open. We were in a room together, the MSN secretive room of love.

> *Dearest Runt,*
>
> *My name is not important – you must know that I am imprisoned and guarded by many jailers – indeed this letter had to be smuggled; if the jailers knew, serious consequences would follow. Yet Disco is a caring person who will write once released. You will know once it happens – but for now thank you.*
> *Pig*

My heart raced and my stomach flipped over. This was the person who I had longed for, for over six months, the one I had dreamed about, the one who I had searched for and now he was here, right next to me in cyber space. I took a deep breath, confused. And as I fleetingly considered whether this person was even sane, I reached for the mouse and began to type my response.

I paused momentarily to think this one through. Was he at work and sending this? Did I have to be careful in my response? Should I sleep on it and leave it till the following day to reply? After all the things that I had said and sent to him, I was hardly worried that he would think I was being pushy or easy. Of course I couldn't help myself; adjourning anything, particularly matters of the heart, was never my strong point.

Dear Pig,

> *Is this really you, are you really the person that I think you are? Oh, I'm so happy. You came, you came to get me! I always knew that you loved me. I could sense it in your voice. You were the one that cared when no one else did; you were the only one who took time out to listen to me without getting angry, stressed or confused. You were there with me in my maddest and silliest moments and you challenged me in my thoughts of suicide. And they took you away from me. The bastards took you from me. God, I have missed you.*
>
> *But I'm afraid, too, because good things never happen to me. If you are not who I think you are then I will be sad and confused and I don't want any more pain. I'm so stupid and ugly, my body is smashed and my life is in pieces. I am one big mess. By the way there are no Discos in this. You are Pig and I am Runt, get it!*
>
> *With regards,*
>
> *Runt*

I hesitated before I sent it as, although I knew this had to be Barry, I wondered if someone had sent it to cheer me up, although that would have felt more like cruelty. A click of the mouse and it was sent. There was no going back now; the lines of communication were wide open.

Dear Runt

> *Pig sees Runt very differently to be honest and sees capabilities and certainly not ugly. Pig also believes good things can happen to people of all descriptions so in addition to the stories it seems a good thing to start to help good things to*

happen to Runt. There was a picture on this profile of a
woman at a wedding – was that Runt? If so ugly is the last
word Pig would use
  Love Pig

I lay down on my bed, thoughts and feelings racing. Scared, excited, anxious, confused overwhelmed and happy. In the middle of all the despair, there was a glimmer of hope, a feeling that something beautiful beyond all belief could indeed happen. I just had to get myself beyond the reality check. Whether I liked it or not, I needed to find out who Barry really was. The thought of this moving from the place where it had been scared me. It sat just where I wanted it to sit, I had loved Barry and I only knew four things about him. 'They', his clinical supervisors, had taken him away from me and I still loved him, now he was here and all was about to be revealed and I wasn't sure I wanted the bubble I had created to burst. This would change things and I didn't like change, my dreams and illusions felt safe and I didn't know whether I wanted to exchange them for the truth. This was the end of something I could control and the start of something someone else had some control over. Moving from my solo monologues towards more of a symmetric multiprocessing was going to be hard. Two-way communications were difficult at the best of times, fantasies and stories felt warmer and safer. I had loved Barry with freedom. In my own little world, my disinhibited love had no rules, no restrictions. We could be together wherever and whenever I wanted it. He had no part in that play but that was no concern of mine. My love for Barry had made me feel complete whilst keeping my unique separateness intact. Loving Barry had helped me to reconnect me back with myself.

I knew I had to do this, I did have a desire to find out who he really was, what he looked like, whether he was married or not, most of all I wanted to know had he felt what I had felt all those months ago when he first took my call. Had he loved me from the first time he heard my voice like I had loved him? Could he read my mind? Did he feel my pain? Did he feel my solitude and desperation during those dark months? Did he want to come to me and caress me when I was in Oxford and save me from myself?

I also owed this to friends who had patiently listened as I rambled on about Barry to them. Barry this, Barry that. Barry had been the sole conversation for the last eight months. Most had listened tentatively; some went along with the idea that Barry loved me; some positively believed that he was the one, while others laughed at the absurdity of it and ridiculed me. My friend's parents with Alzheimer's never got fed up of me though, 'Oh, that's a lovely story my dear, what did you say love? Tell me again.' I visited them frequently and discussed all four things I knew about Barry over and over again and no one seemed to mind.

Something had changed and, although I was aware of it, I couldn't name it. Something felt different. I felt less manic, more stable, maybe less in love with Barry and maybe more certain of who I was. I hadn't felt like this for years. Everything felt different, tangible almost, genuine and true. I had become one-dimensional working in child protection, operating with detachment and void of all feeling, having no time to heal from one serious situation to the next. No one talked about horrors we witnessed or the neglect and abuse inflicted upon the children we worked with.

The next day, I hobbled to the computer. Physically things weren't getting better but coping was made easier now I had my muse back. No mail. My heart sank. No mail all day. In the evening, I visited a friend in my new wheelchair, nearly tipping myself out of it twice despite only wheeling myself five doors up. When I got back home, I sat back at the computer desk. The chair was hard and everything hurt and I had had a few drinks too many.

Too much booze, too much and far too much Eva Cassidy, again! Moments later I started again…

Dear Pig

I have written a number of poems for you and you can access them at LovingYou.com under the name of Drew Jellyfields. I will send you a few sample poems. Caution there may be swearing and there are many that are very rude to you, but don't worry the majority are love poems. There are approximately 492 altogether. I hope that you don't feel too overwhelmed by this.

I'm feeling very scared at the moment and very vulnerable. You have seen a picture of me and heard me in my full glory over many months this year having a nervous breakdown over the phone and you know all my intimate details, even when my periods are due, and I know nothing of you. I have an image in my head of what you look like. I feel very naked at the moment, like my whole life has become public knowledge, a soap opera.

Regards Runt

Moments later I received a reply. I wasn't as excited as I would have expected. Momentarily I considered whether I was in fact getting better mentally. It was becoming clear to me that my obsession or crush on Barry was symptomatic of my illness, a by-product of being bipolar. It was a macabre fairy tale, one that had had devastating consequences for me personally. Irrespective of that I was still very pleased that Barry had replied. His response was cooler and slightly more distant.

Dear Runt

Your intensity of feeling is very obvious and clear and, for me, a little overwhelming at the moment. Yes, you do have to meet me, which will happen for certain – I guess you will have to decide what to do if you do not find me attractive as that will call for a reassessment I guess! I liked the poems – I looked at the ones you sent me and also noted that you wrote them ages ago too – so thank you for sending those

What you got planned for the rest of the day?

Dear Pig

I want to make love to you and I trust you and I'll let you decide how best to deal with that situation, Bazza. I do actually have to meet with you first though but what if I don't find you attractive? Not that that really matters to me actually, cos I know how I feel about you anyway. Hope you like my poems.

P.S. I'm sorry that I overwhelm you, I can't help it. I am a Nut Job.

Love Runt

Dear Runt

No need to apologise about the overwhelming thing – if I ever want to respond to you I want it to be something out of me and not simply something I see in you, if that makes sense. In addition, you don't need to be sexual to get my attention, you already have it. As for meeting me like you are now, I don't mind meeting you in whatever state you are. It certainly would not put you off me.

The emails continued for days, fifteen to twenty sent and received each day. I felt happy inside but also slightly worried. I wondered whether Barry was a safe man, which was something I hadn't thought of before. I started to give some real consideration to the fact that I didn't really know anything about him and that he could actually be a mad man.

We stopped using piggy names and started to use our own names. This felt odd as it took it out of the context that I was comfortable with, like a play with actors. He had started to seem more real now, like a proper person: real in a way that I had not imagined before.

Dear Barry

Do you think this is sustainable, at some stage I am going to have to see what you look like.

Love Kathryn x

Hi wonderful,

I can't see any reason why it can't be sustainable – look how long you have been waiting already! Spiritually I feel called to the Dorset area (which includes Hampshire as far as I can see) but now am pulled to South Yorkshire for some strange reason.

It will be sustainable for other reasons too – this 'pull' that we feel will only get stronger and intensified once we join together sexually – and I only wish I could come to you now but we need to wait and get that sorted I know.

You have turned my world upside down that is for sure – it is hard to see how I can be anyone's other than yours; certainly if our meeting goes as well as everything else seems to be doing at the moment – best way I can think of to start the New Year.

Love Barry

I took a deep breath. *He really does love me,* I thought to myself. I was starting to get a bit worried. It all seemed to be running away with me, but I was still playing the game because I didn't know how to stop it, I didn't know if I wanted it to stop. It just wasn't supposed to happen this way. He was meant to come and get me before I jumped off the building...

You're a little late Barry, I'm already torn, I thought to myself.

I wondered what he really wanted with me? Money? I started to consider my position in grown-up terms. I am vulnerable as I can't walk, I am mental and I own my own home: those were all things he knew about me.

That night, Barry phoned, which had also now become the norm. We had become connected on the phone again and at first it was great. His soft, gentle voice lulled me and I felt warm and safe, but I wondered – and never so strongly as I wondered it now – who the face was behind the phone?

My darling Kathryn

The warmth of darkness surrounds me as I recline in my bed
Mind full of thoughts like electric shocks explode into my consciousness

As I try to make sense of one explosion another happens, so that I never really recover in time to cope with the ecstasy of the first, I hardly have time to become accustomed to these new sensations.

When I become aware that there are feelings inside me that I hardly dare believe
For they are feelings that rock my heart and make my pulse race
Feelings that as they spread bring great joy mingled with disbelief

Can this really be true?

Fear and trepidation and disbelief flow equally – what could this divine being see in me – me who in comparison am but nothing?
For you my love are the creator of all these things and more – who else could make me record such words?

Tears now brim as I think of you and all that has passed without me – how much longer can I live without your daily presence? Quench my thirst and return my love!
   Love Barry

That threw me completely. I was not expecting that response at all. Barry was meant to be distant, sophisticated, mysterious and aloof. He was giving away too much of himself and I didn't know what to do now. The crazy poetry was never meant to be reciprocated! My crap poetry was crap because I was ill. Had I sent Barry into Mentaldom?

Dear Runt
   It is only in the last few days that I have made sense of everything and can put a name to what I have been going through
   Too long have I strained my eyes to peer through mists
   Ever grasping at shadows believing them to be you
   But now that you are truly revealed and my heart has disclosed its long held secrets, I can truthfully say that I want to be with no other.

More booze needed!

Dear Bazza
   If you are the true one that I have been searching for, then

215

what will come will be beautiful I promise you that. If you are the one that my body has long awaited then your dreams will be made real. If you are the one whom will keep me warm, then I will cherish you for eternity.

Love me x

My Dearest Runt (Pig names resumed)

Many spiritual paths have identified love as being at the heart of all that matters. The world over is affected by it and made better for it.

Yet it is an elusive feeling so easily confused with others – certainly for me as I have tried to keep those important boundaries in place. Hammering the lid shut upon what stirred within, yet only in these last weeks did I realise that my spiritual perspectives were more important and that you had to come first no matter what – the lid began to be prised open and the feelings began to escape.

Still unsure as to how to describe them, petrified of sending you away scared, longing for you with a longing so strong that I should risk all just to follow my heart and spirit.

And yet it was you, with your certainty that you love me, with your insight so razor sharp that exposed me with nowhere to hide and to face the only conclusion I can.

That what I feel is love – love for you as you are. Wanting to share love with you. Standing face-to-face, eye-to-eye, seeing your pupils dilate in response to my love showered upon you, the very ether trembling as we both dare hope that what has so long been dreamed of should come into being.

For You from Me

I was concerned that I was taking this person who I didn't even know deeper and deeper into a world that I had created when I was sick, and that his life was being turned upside down because of me. I didn't want him to get hurt in this and needed to bring it to its conclusion. Barry had informed me he had a partner, but had played it down saying they were just friends. Her name was Mary and they had lived together for the last four years. He explained that they had been growing apart for some time.

I was concerned that I was the reason for their recent distance. Barry had shared his home number with me so that I could contact him at any time. Mary occasionally answered the phone and appeared to accept me as his 'special friend'. She would always be polite in asking if I was alright, and happy to pass me onto Barry.

Dear Runt

I can appreciate that this is scary and you feel unsafe, and that is the last thing I want to happen for you. The way I see it is this:

You have been far more sensitive than I have. I was bound up by trying to make sense of your illness, by sticking to the counselling ethics and yet at the same time having to cope with the pull your way.

I was determined, also, to be faithful and was therefore in a difficult situation – having this strong attraction to you and yet not being able to do anything about it. Do I believe you love me? Yes I do, even though in the eyes of the world it makes no sense at all, just as my response makes no sense.

Getting in touch with you was the catalyst that forced Mary and I to break immediately – not in any horrible way but simply a realisation that the reason we had been brought together was over. By the way, we have also agreed to no sexual contact – that would only be confusing and she prefers women anyway.

There is a bit in the Bible where someone had the truth revealed to them and it is described as scales falling away from their eyes – I feel like that with you – once I saw things in context I understood.

So, what now between you and me? It seems to me that it is important for you to recover your health in all its aspects so that you can re-establish your career so, although you offered to move to me now is not the time, which means that I need to move to you because I cannot cope with the distance etc. It will take me time to get there, probably a minimum of three months I suppose, so there is no hurry in any respect.

Thanks once again for letting me talk with you – it is really hard trying to keep my feet on the ground and just wait for you to get in touch with me; fortunately I am short of cash this month otherwise I would have driven up by now.

Lots of love

Your darling!

★

It was my best friend, Walt's birthday and my friends had agreed to take me out with them. No one was very good at pushing wheelchairs. We got a taxi and went for a meal at the local curry house. That evening I felt so happy to be alive and included and despite the agony I felt well, and happy that I was surrounded by the love of my friends.

I had missed being me. It had been such a long time since I had last seen or spoken to myself as a well person, and I liked who I was becoming. More settled and able to listen rather than talk, more confident with my place in the world and happy that I was simply alive.

Emotions were running high in my friendship circle. The 'incident' had impacted everyone. No one could have ever imagined something like this happening. My friends had started to look at their own lives and put into perspective their petty disagreements and problems, prioritising family and friends over working endless hours for little return. I could feel a natural progression of reaffirmation of all our love for each other, that we were special and lucky to have one another. It made all of us wake up and realise the importance of what we all had.

*

Dear Kathryn

Good morning. Hope your outing went well and that you slept well. I have decided to attach a picture of myself for you to see as I do not want our relationship to continue without you seeing what I look like.

It seems to me that what we might agree on is that there is potential for more in our relationship, and in the process of discovery it will either be confirmed that we can go further or we will be put off from forming an intimate relationship even though friendship is something I would want to maintain.

So instead of asking you to tell me how you felt yesterday I should have asked if there was sufficient to give a relationship a try – so I am sorry for getting that one wrong :)

Ah well I could go on rambling but I have to be at work for midday – I will look forward to hearing from you if you feel like it and if not then I will be thinking of you

xxxx

Dear Barry

May I take this opportunity to thank you for your picture. You are a very interesting-looking person; you look very similar to Jim Royle, Ricky Tomlinson from the Royle Family on television.

There is something that you need to understand, Barry, I do have a tendency to live in a dream world, a world where I can easily create a fantasy or illusion and live out that illusion in all its glory, I think that this may be a symptom of my illness. I mentioned earlier that it really didn't matter what you looked like as I would love and accept you no matter what. I am deeply sorry to have to say this but I no longer think that we are spiritually connected. I am really sorry. I hope that we can be friends.

Regards Runt

Dearest Runt

I am feeling a little battered and bruised because of everything. I want to be friends with you too but I have taken on board what you said yesterday – maybe we both need to concentrate on different things. I do not want to get into a relationship if you are not the person for me so will be looking everywhere, not just Sheffield, for work – I can of course travel to see you if that is ever an issue

Take care x

It was time for a deep 'let go'. I had given up the old me and was beginning to accept that this was my new life. I had given up on trying to make everything better, trying to improve things that I had little or no effect over. I was trying to accept that there was nothing more that I could do other than to allow life to play itself out the way it was going to, day by day. I felt reborn like I had been given a second chance, a chance to see the world from a different vantage point and I began cherishing each moment that I had on the planet.

That very night, I became enlightened.

FIFTEEN

To Infinity and Beyond

ONE MONTH AFTER DISCHARGE MY psychiatrist, in a panic, made several referrals for a wide range of different support options that should have been offered before I jumped. One of those referrals was for marriage guidance counselling, which made no sense at all, given that I had never been married and was not in a relationship.

Two weeks after Barry showed me his photograph I met Alex, who became my partner and lived with me for five years. Alex and I had been to university together some twelve years before and he had returned from Cuba where he had lived for three years. A mutual friend brought him to see me and we spent the evening laughing and telling each other stories on my bed until dawn. Alex became my rock.

Four months after discharge I began volunteering at First Trust Mental Health Charity in Sheffield. It was around this time that an appointment was offered with a psychologist.

Six months after discharge I embarked on a business school training course with REGEN School to learn how to set up a Social Enterprise.

One year after discharge – I set up 'FlippinMental' a self-help group and service user training agency to both support peers and educate professionals, students at university and other agencies on the impact of mental illness.

It was also around this time that my therapy ended with the mental health team and I was given a diagram of what the psychologist thought were the issues. It looked extremely similar to two other people's diagrams. They also had bipolar and were friends of mine from the group. It resembled nothing about my life and my experiences and I tore it up and threw it in the bin after leaving their office.

Three years after my incident I became a grandma to the second most beautiful person in my life, Jack. Jack has autism.

Five years after my incident I embarked on the 'Storying Sheffield' course run by Professor Brendan Stone at Sheffield University. This gave me an ideal opportunity to tell my story using conceptual art. I had nine pieces of art in that exhibition and on the day of the final exhibition I was told I had been successful in gaining paid employment with a local charity. This was also the first time I had been near the building I jumped off.

The post I was offered at Disability Sheffield was an advocate for disabled people. This gave me a real opportunity to help give a voice to people that so often are misunderstood and misrepresented. My confidence started to be rebuilt and the role put me in direct touch with the disability community, a community I am the most at home with.

Seven years after my incident I came off Olanzapine, the anti-psychotic drug that had caused me to gain over nine stone in weight. It was extremely traumatic coming off this medication as it imitated an episode. I rode it through the Christmas of 2010 and went through 'cold turkey' without the mayonnaise. It is my belief that I should never have been left on this medication for so long and that just because a person is experiencing a mental health episode, it doesn't mean that they are unwell forever.

Eight years after my incident I had my fourteenth operation

to remove some metal work from my leg and replace my hip which had exploded out of my body on impact. It was during this hospital stay that I found out my good friend Martin had died from a possible hit-and-run accident only weeks earlier in Wakefield. Martin and I had placed bets on who was going to die first after leaving hospital. He had had a run of good things happen to him after he was discharged two months after me in 2005, and he had achieved miracles. Sadly this was followed by a run of bad luck and Martin had ended up back on drugs three years later.

Hands down I had won the bet.

Nine years after discharge, I was given the opportunity to work as a new employment development worker. This entailed designing and delivering training to health and social care staff around issues of employment and disability as part of the wider employment strategy. This was the pinnacle of my journey so far and it provided me with an opportunity to use my own experiences positively to explore the issues and impact of mental illness and disability on both the individual and wider society in terms of work, which is central to most people's lives. I was able to positively challenge the low aspirations for people with lifelong disabilities and impairments with regards to employment, and to support and equip services with the tools, knowledge and support they needed to adequately and timely support an individual with their employment needs.

In this year I also had two pieces of writing published, one short story in a compendium of narratives *Our Encounters with Suicide* by Brendan Stone, Judith Haire, Fran Biley and Alec Grant and a short piece in a book for Bipolar UK, *30 Years of Bipolar*.

Ten years after discharge, I am mentally stable and medication-free. Barry and I are still in touch, despite the fact we have never seen or met each other. We speak on the phone regularly and, although he knows he will never be as funny as me, he continues to enjoy my sadomasochistic approach to our phone conversations. He still gets called a colourful range of obscenities if he is unable to satisfy all of my immediate demands.

Barry and I are in touch on a regular basis. He is both my friend and my supporter and I know that, if I ever need anything, he will be there. And just by knowing that, I feel safe. I know that Barry loves me and I him, in a nonromantic way of course. We are in agreement that this is undoubtedly the longest non-relationship that either of us has ever had. On the 25th November each year, Barry has a whole day where we celebrate his contributions to my life. Usually I turn my phone off. Do I think that Barry stepped over his professional boundaries? Yes, probably he did but in this instance I am glad he did because he helped me to heal and to find my own way back to myself.

I have a wonderful relationship with my daughter, Faye, who has developed into an intelligent, empathetic young woman who completely understands my experiences and no longer blames me for the trauma she experienced.

I continue to see my orthopedic surgeons, Mr Kerry and Mr Blundell who treat me with the utmost respect. They are afraid to discharge me as they are far too interested in my life and what I might do next. In 2012 I wrote Mr Kerry a little book about him, for him, titled *The Wibbly Woman Woman*. Never before had replacing hips been so much fun for him.

People often ask, 'Do you regret jumping off a building?'

My answer to that is quite simply 'no'. To regret this incident would be an admission that a conscious decision was taken to determine the ultimate action. How can an incident like this not be an illness? My incident was, in no uncertain terms, caused by serious mental illness exasperated by acute stress levels working in the chronically under resourced area of child protection. No one can know for sure why some people become so unwell and some people don't. I only know that, without this incident taking place, and without having the amazing gift of being bipolar, I would not have this amazing life that is so rich with experience, deep understanding and insight. I am an extremely lucky person and I dedicate this book to all those who have suffered and did not make it.